Your 2nd DSLR & The Workhorse DSLR

Shawn M. Tomlinson's
Guide to Photography
Volumes 7 & 8

by

shawn m tomlinson

2015

Your 2nd DSLR & The Workhorse DSLR

*Shawn M. Tomlinson's
Guide to Photography
Volumes 7 & 8*

ISBN: 978-1-329-39652-4

Cover photo © 2014, 2015 by
Gary W. Ziroli

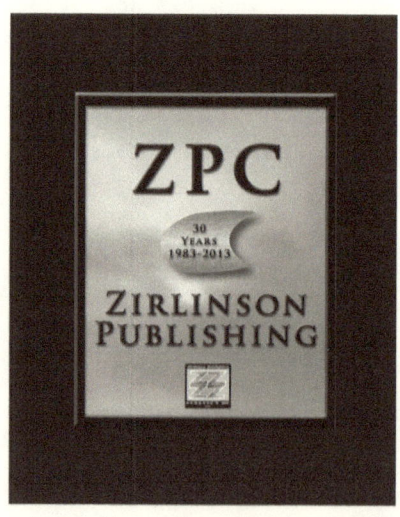

Contents

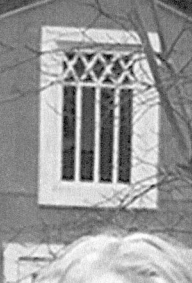

Your 2nd DSLR

How & Why To Buy a 2nd Camera Body

Shawn M. Tomlinson's Guide to Photography Volume 7

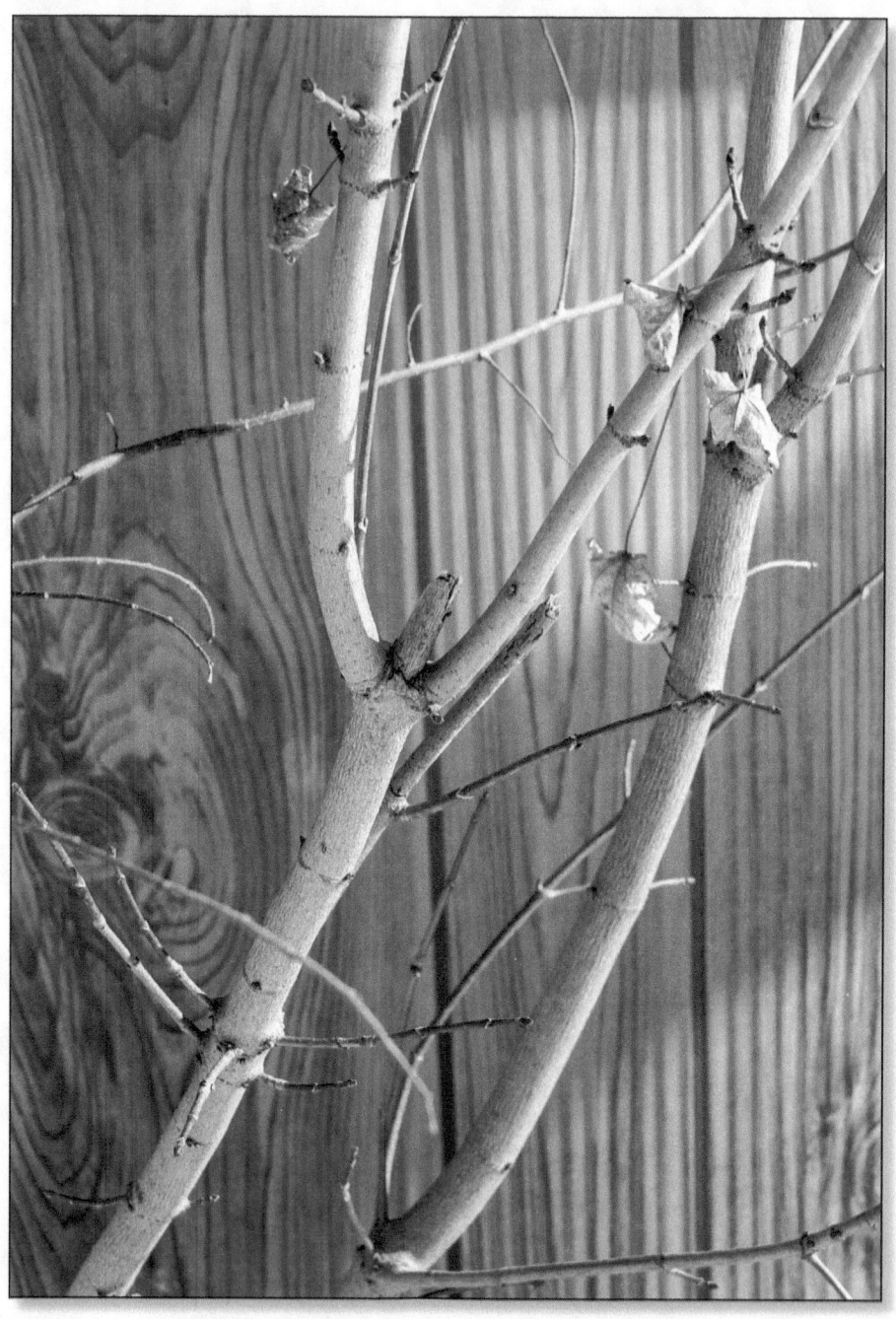

Ballston Lake, N.Y., Feb. 4, 2014.
Nikon D70, 80mm, 1/250, f/9, ISO 200, P, pattern metering
Photo © 2014, 2015 by Shawn M. Tomlinson

First Words

It is time, the photographer said, to speak of many things; of lenses and filters and gadget bags and things.

Not exactly what Lewis Carroll wrote, but it'll do. He was a photographer, too, so he might approve of the paraphrase.

The consideration here, though, is not lenses, filters or gadget bags.

It is the acquisition of a second digital single-lens reflex camera to add to your photographer's arsenal.

There are many reasons to get a second DSLR, well, four main ones:

1. Upgrade. DSLR technology changes rapidly and even if you bought the latest, greatest camera two years ago, it has likely been superseded by a newer, usually better model.

2. Experiment. You may be fairly happy with your DSLR brand, but what of those others? Why do people buy the brands you chose not to? Maybe it's time to find out.

3. Backup. It's frustrating and embarrassing to be in the middle of a shoot and your DSLR packs it in. A second DSLR in your gadget bag can come to

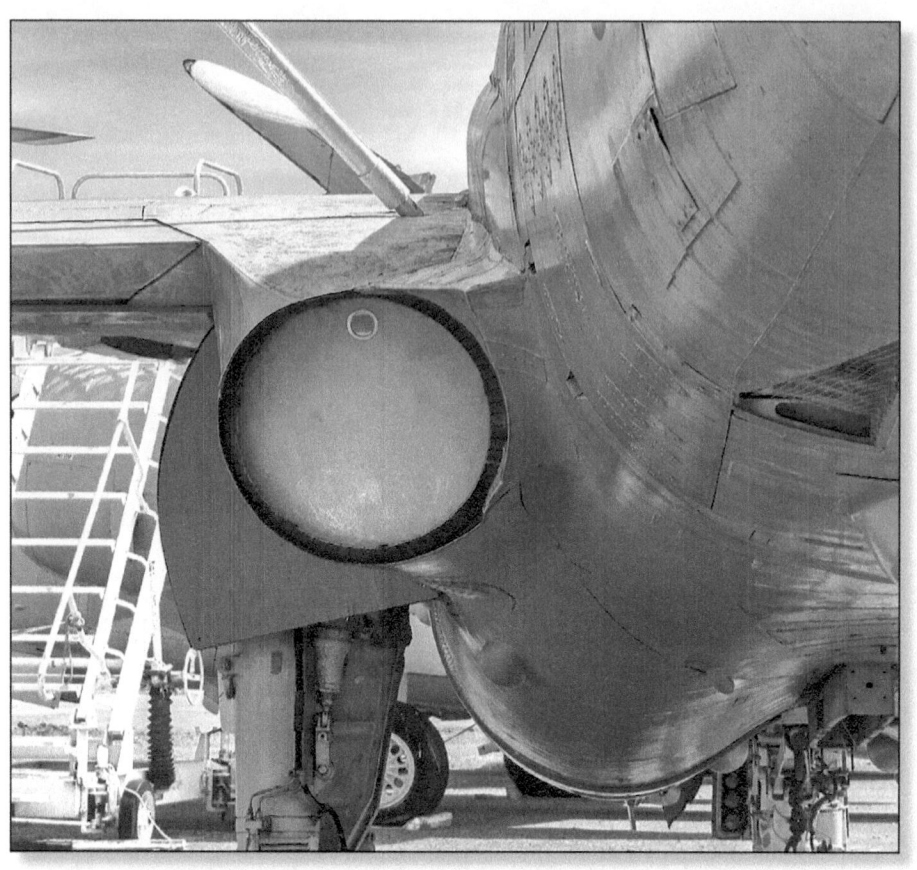

Air Museum, Glenville, N.Y., April 20, 2014.
Nikon D70, 66mm, 1/400, f/10, ISO 200, P, pattern metering
Photo © 2014, 2015 by Shawn M. Tomlinson

the rescue.

4. Going Pro. You're making good money shooting on the weekends, so it's time to think about turning professional. You will need more than one DSLR camera.

There's also a fifth reason, and one that most likely has crossed your mind.

You may be considering a second DSLR just because, well, you want one.

This book explores these considerations and makes some recommendations to help you in your next step as a photographer.

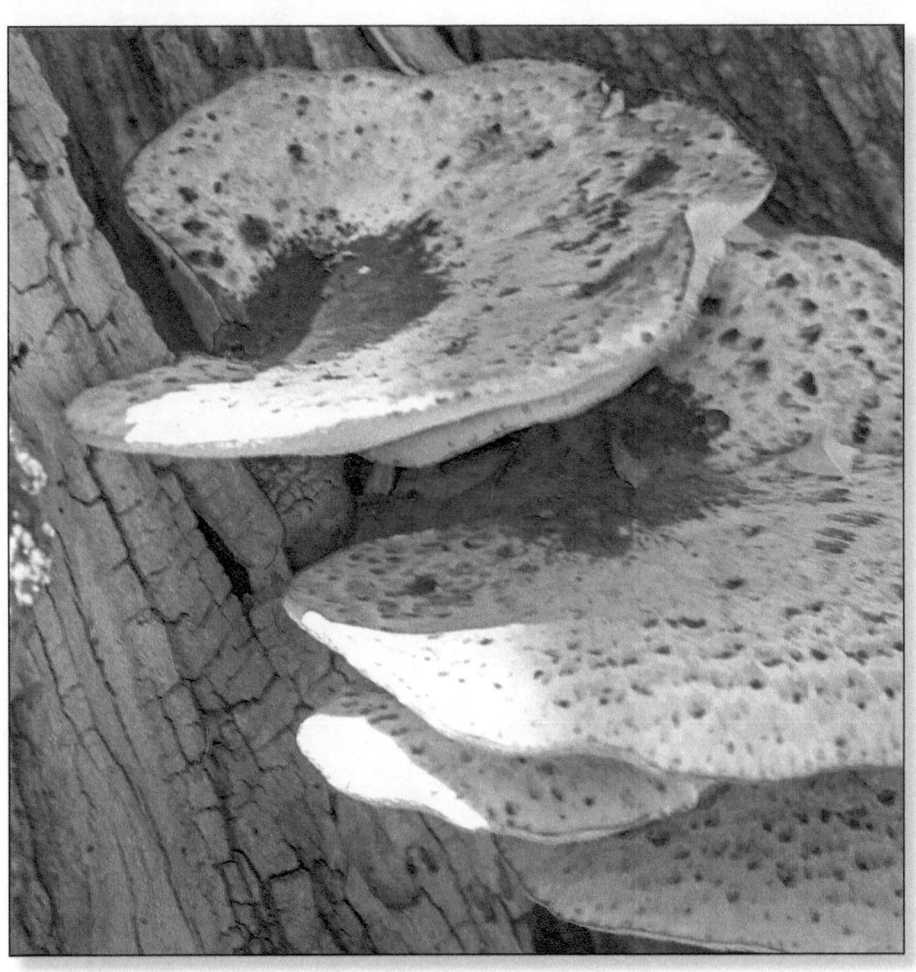

Clarksville, NY, June 8, 2014
Canon EOS 20D, 69mm, 1/60, f/5.6, ISO 200, P, pattern metering
© 2014, 2015 by Shawn M. Tomlinson

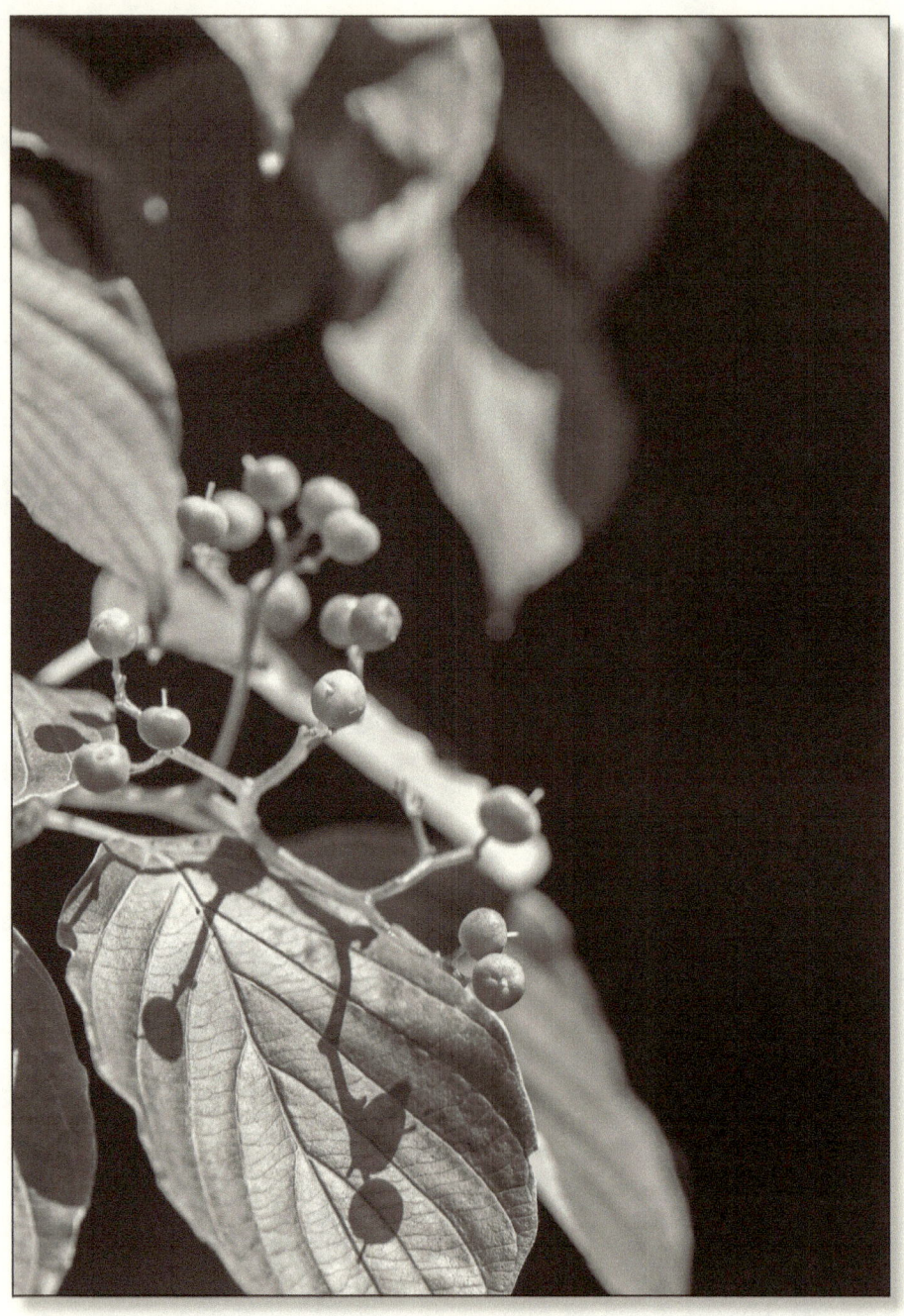

Saratoga Springs, NY, July 11, 2015
Nikon D800e, 105mm, 1/500, f/4, ISO 200, S, pattern metering
© 2015 by Shawn M. Tomlinson

Reason 1
Upgrading

This probably is the most obvious reason a photographer considers buying a second DSLR.

We are a society of everything newer is better, even when that isn't true. So, sure, I just bought a spiffy, shiny DSLR, but, ooo, what's *that* one like? It's newer so it must be better.

In general, that is true as long as you stay within

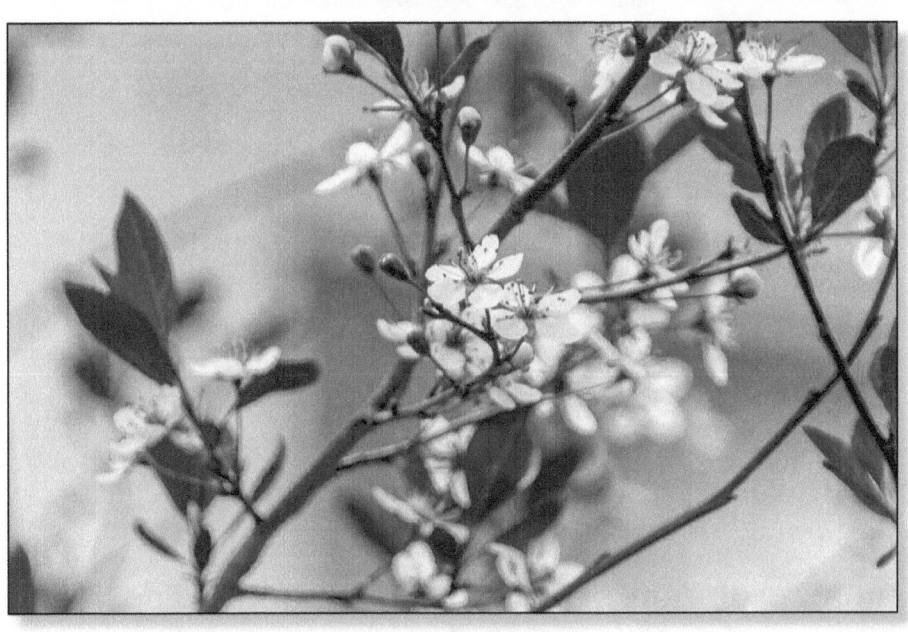

Ballston Lake, N.Y., May 13, 2014.
Canon EOS 20D, 200mm, 1/320, f/5.6, ISO 200, Tv, average metering
Photo © 2014, 2015 by Shawn M. Tomlinson

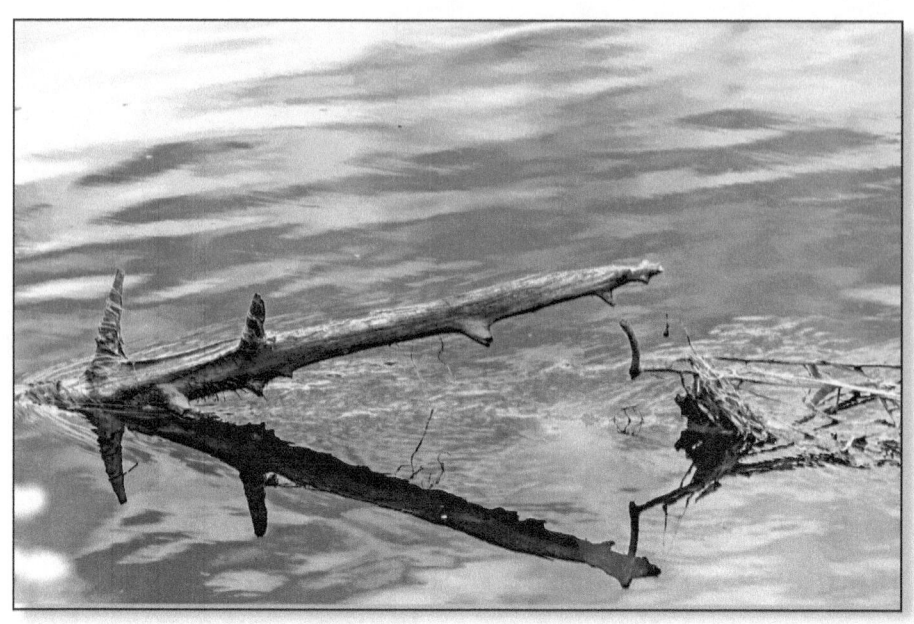

Fort Edward, N.Y., Aug. 9, 2014.
Nikon D1, 300mm, 1/500, f/5.6, ISO 200, Av, pattern metering
Photo © 2014, 2015 by Shawn M. Tomlinson

the DSLR class to which you already belong.

For example, if you have a Nikon D200, a Nikon D300 is a definite upgrade. They both are semi-pro DSLRs, so they both have solid builds and semi-pro controls. There's a slight resolution bump between them, but more importantly, the D300 has Nikon's Active-D Lighting thingy that really brings out details in bright and shadow areas.

However, if you have a Nikon D200, a Nikon D3200 isn't really an upgrade. The latter does have more resolution, but it is cheaply built and designed for entry-level, so it will frustrate you. It feels drastically plasticy and the LCD on the top right is missing. It has little scene pictographs on the Mode dial you'll never use — thankfully — and it just doesn't seem that great.

As another example, the Canon EOS 20D was such a fantastic camera that the company made only slight upgrades to it through the 30D, 40D and 50D. It

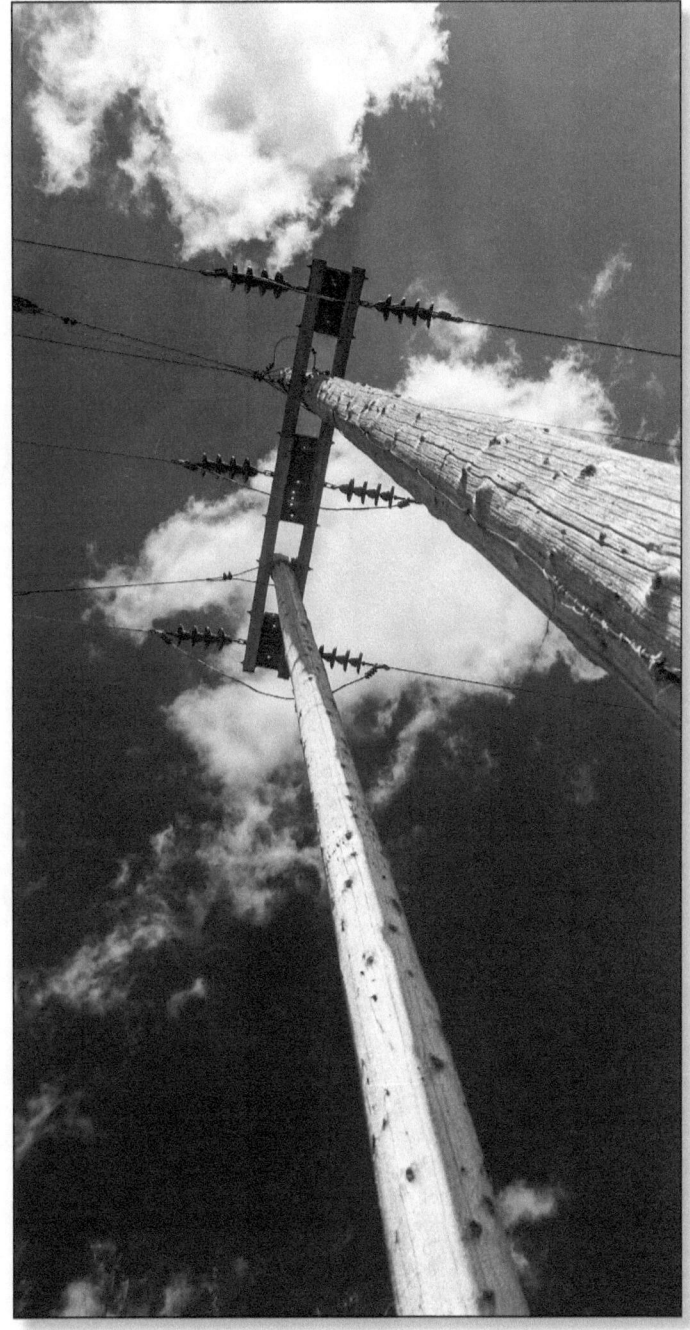

Glens Falls, N.Y., April 19, 2014.
Pentax K20D, 18mm, 1/3000, f/5.6, ISO 280, P, pattern metering
Photo © 2014, 2015 by Shawn M. Tomlinson

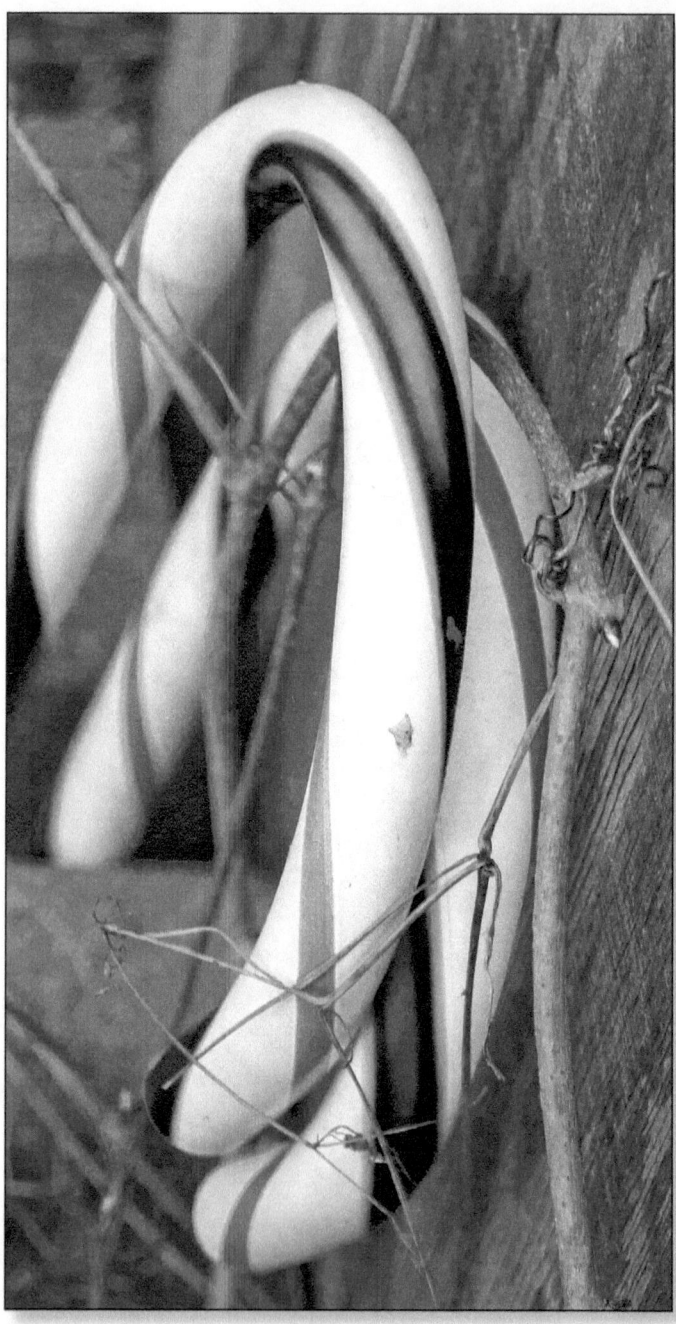

Ballston Lake, N.Y., April 25, 2014.
Canon EOS 20D, 80mm, 1/125, f/6.3, ISO 400, P, pattern metering
Photo © 2014, 2015 by Shawn M. Tomlinson

wasn't until the 70D that things changed quite a bit. So, is it worth it to upgrade to a 30D or 40D from a 20D? The resolution is the same between the 20D and 30D, and only gets a slight increase in the 40D.

Higher megapixel counts don't matter that much anyway, despite what camera salespeople or glaring advertisements may tell you. My 20D has 8.2 megapixels, roughly a third of Nikon's entry-level cameras, yet I get such great images from it, I'm in no hurry to replace it. I only bought the 20D to replace my 10D because the 10D died in the middle of a shoot.

OK, six reasons.

Upgrading a DSLR is not as straight forward as it at first appears.

The key to upgrading is to either stay within the same DSLR class and get a newer camera, or to move up to the next DSLR class. So, for example, if you have a Pentax K-X, it might be time to grad-

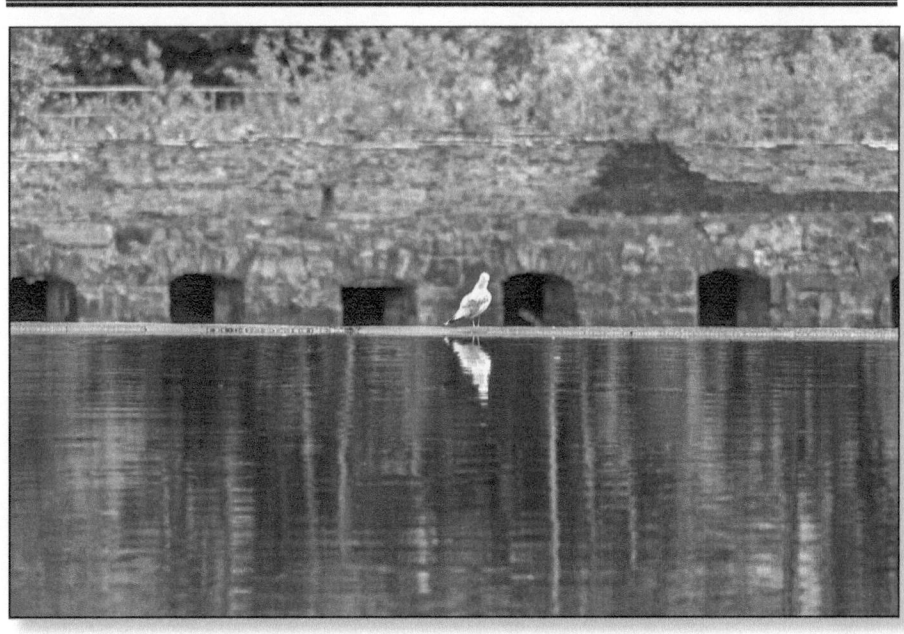

Fort Edward, N.Y., Aug. 9, 2014.
Nikon D1, 270mm, 1/1000, f/5.3, ISO 200, Tv, pattern metering
Photo © 2014, 2015 by Shawn M. Tomlinson

uate to a Pentax K-5 IIs or a Pentax K-3.

Considerations:

1) Does the newer DSLR model have better features for you?

2) Is it a significant upgrade?

3) Is it worth the money?

4) Would investing in a better lens for your current DSLR be a better idea?

These four points may intrude upon the excitement and enthusiasm of wanting a new DSLR, but they are worth thinking about.

1) Virtually all DSLRs take great photographs according to your own talent and skill. So the main question to consider for an upgrade is: Does the newer/better camera have features that *you* want and will use that your current camera does not?

For example, I really like a feature on older, mid-range Canon DSLRs called A-DEP. It's a dummy feature for photographers too lazy to calculate effective depth-of-field. See, utilizing depth-of-field puts more subjects at different distances in focus in the same shot.

When lenses still had aperture rings, we calculated DOF by focusing upon the farthest thing we wanted in focus and noting the distance number on the lens. Then we focused upon the nearest subject and noted that distance. Lenses also used to have

DOF scales on them, so we looked at this while turning the focusing ring to the middle of the two focus values we noted earlier. These two distances lined up with numbers on the DOF scale. This told us the f-stop we needed to get

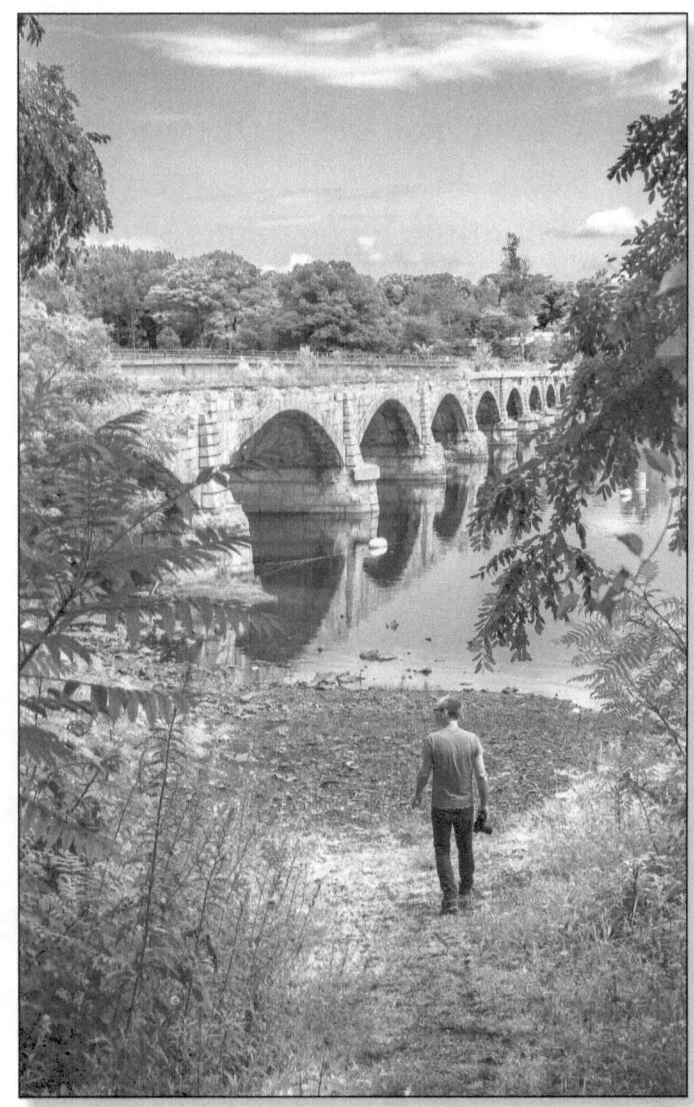

Gary Ziroli, Fort Edward, N.Y., Aug. 9, 2014.
Canon EOS 20D, 28mm, 1/250, f/9, ISO 400, P, pattern metering
Photo © 2014, 2015 by Shawn M. Tomlinson

the correct depth-of-field to get the nearest and farthest subjects in focus.

That's a bit complicated, but it works.

Without the DOF scale and without aperture

rings, it's virtually impossible to do this with any accurate calculation.

So Canons had the A-DEP Mode on their Mode dials. Set it, compose your scene and the camera used its multiple focus points to do all that calculating stuff. Canon cameras still have this Mode, but it's harder to get to, which makes the Canon EOS 20D and a few others better for me when I want to use A-DEP. The elimination of easy access to this Mode makes newer models a little less of use to me.

The point is that, as a photographer, your DSLR is *your* main instrument or tool. You need to be so

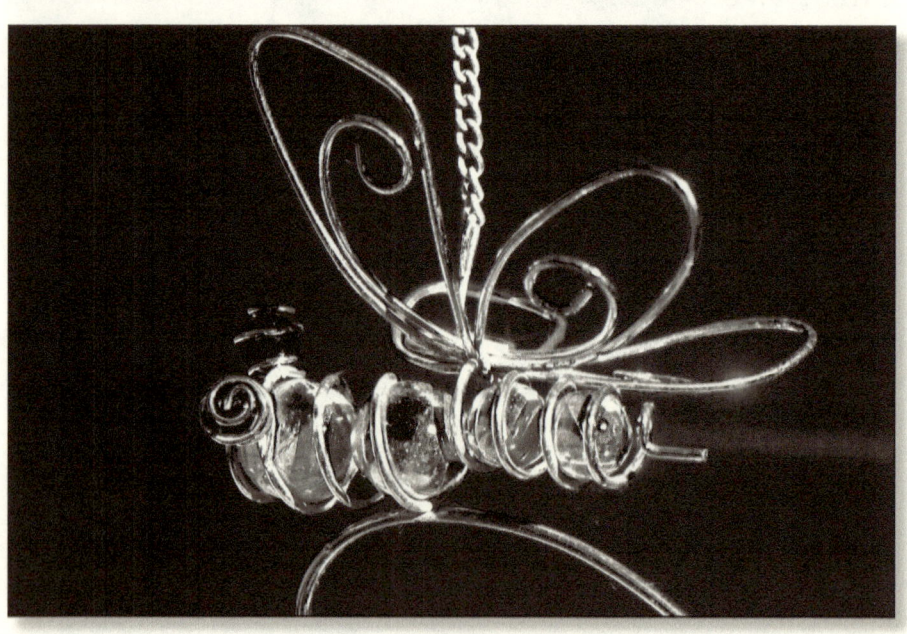

Ballston Lake, N.Y., Nov. 2, 2014.
Nikon D7000, 300mm, 1/1000, f/6.3, ISO 400, Tv, pattern metering
Photo © 2014, 2015 by Shawn M. Tomlinson

familiar with it that it is automatic for you to get it to do what you want. This means it should have the features *you* want where *you* want them, where it is comfortable for you to use them.

Fortunately, through photographer feedback, most camera manufacturers gradually incorporate the features we want into their cameras. Sometimes, though, they eliminate some like the A-DEP mode that makes me reluctant to trade in my Canon EOS 20D.

You need to decide what features you want and which camera comes closest to having them and putting them where you find them easy to get to.

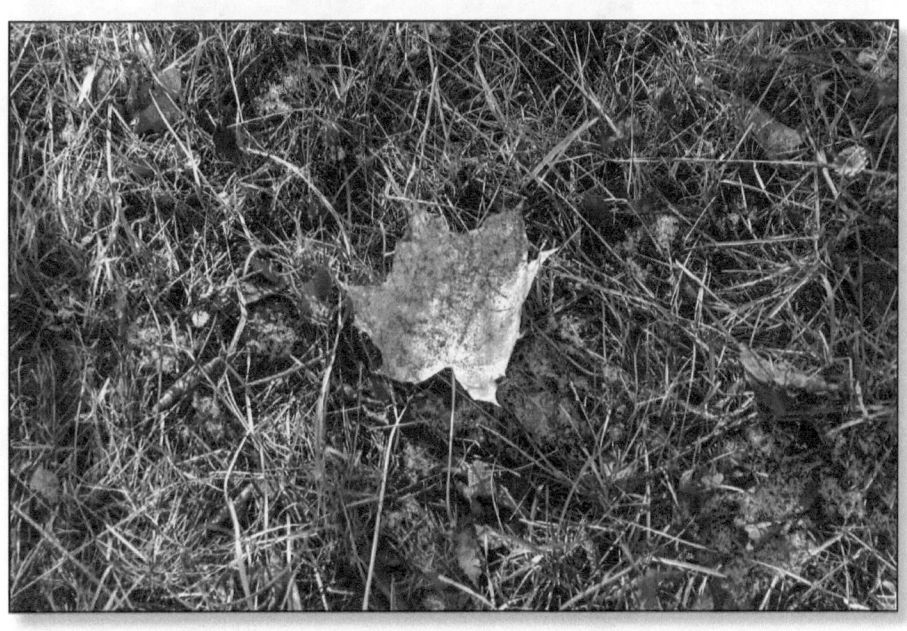

Indian Kill Nature Preserve, Glenville, N.Y., Nov. 15, 2014.
Nikon D7000, 28mm, 1/800, f/2.8, ISO 320, Tv, pattern metering
Photo © 2014, 2015 by Shawn M. Tomlinson

2) Many times manufacturers produce only slight tweaks to their products, renumber them and tout them as significant upgrades. For example, if you already have a Nikon D3300 and you're looking at the Nikon D5300: Both have 24-megapixel resolution and both have nearly identical features and controls. The only difference, real-

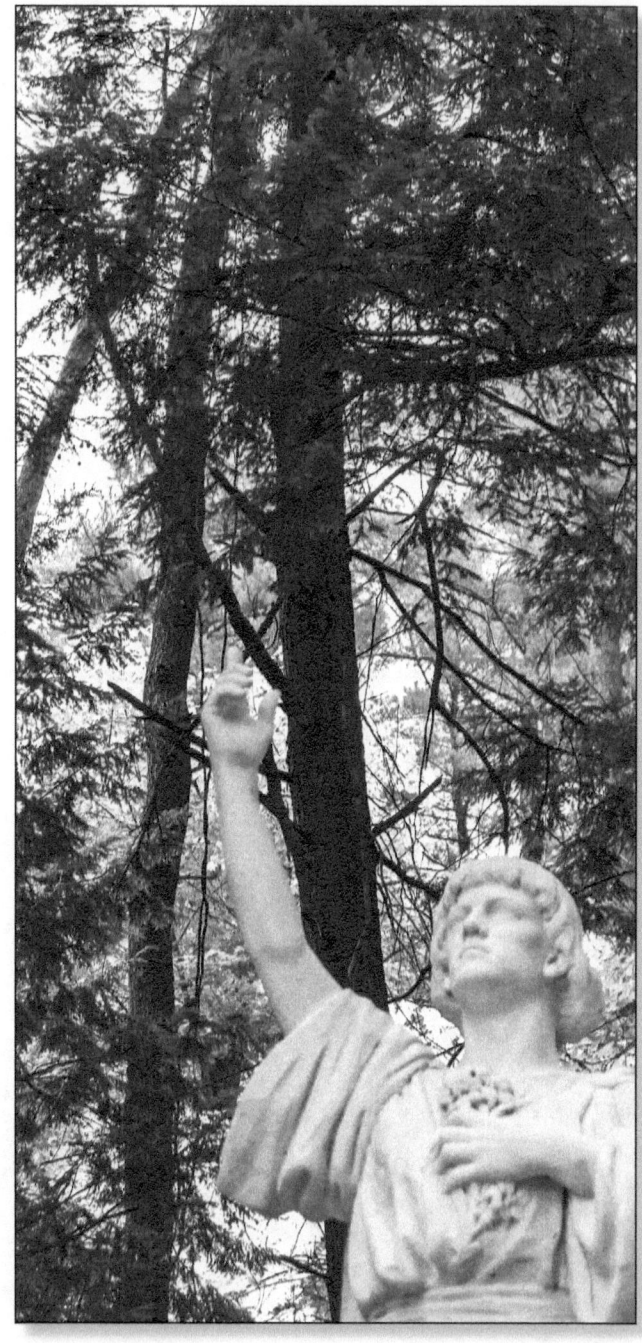

Yaddo, Saratoga Springs, N.Y., Nov. 1, 2014.
Nikon D7000, 55mm, 1/125, f/5.6, ISO 400, Tv, pattern metering
Photo © 2014, 2015 by Shawn M. Tomlinson

ly, is that the D5300 has an articulated — meaning tilty-flippy — rear LCD screen. If that is something you have been bemoaning as missing from the D3300, then by all means, spend the extra money for the D5300. If you think it's just silly, stick with the D3300 or

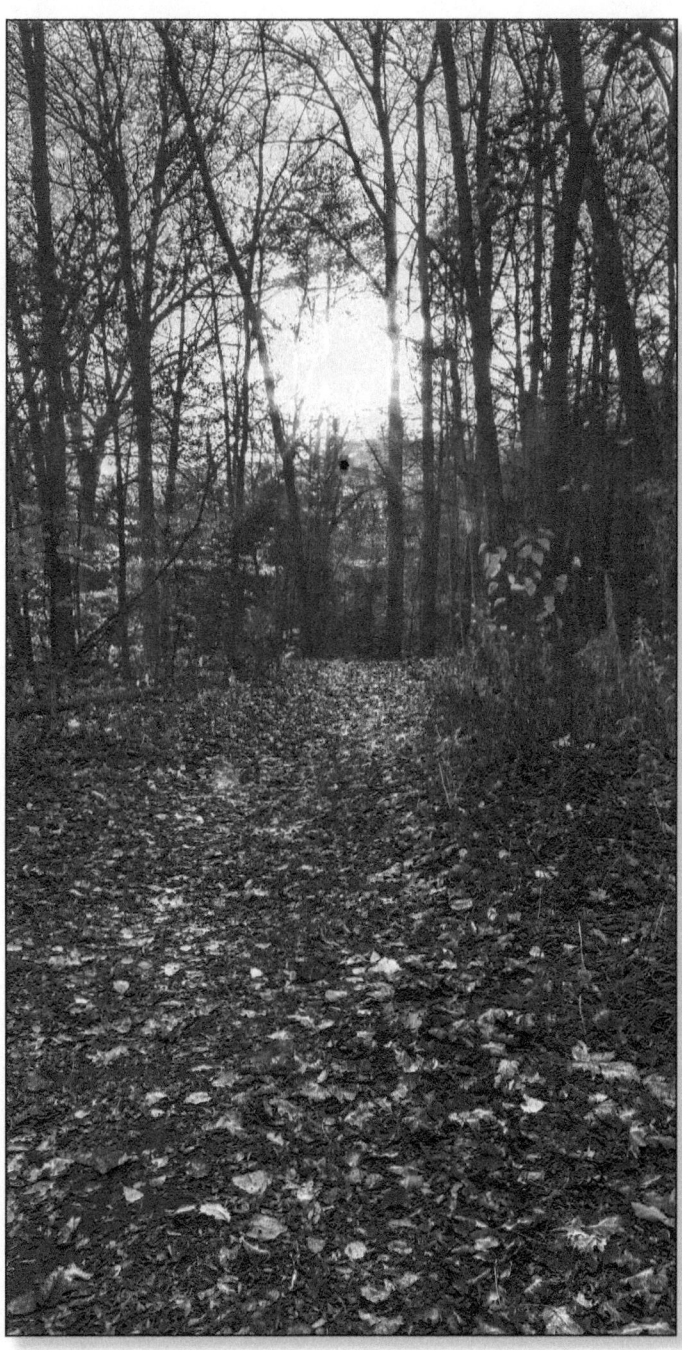

Indian Kill Nature Preserve, Glenville, N.Y., Nov. 4, 2014.
Nikon D7000, 18mm, 1/100, f/22, ISO 400, Tv, pattern metering
Photo © 2014, 2015 by Shawn M. Tomlinson

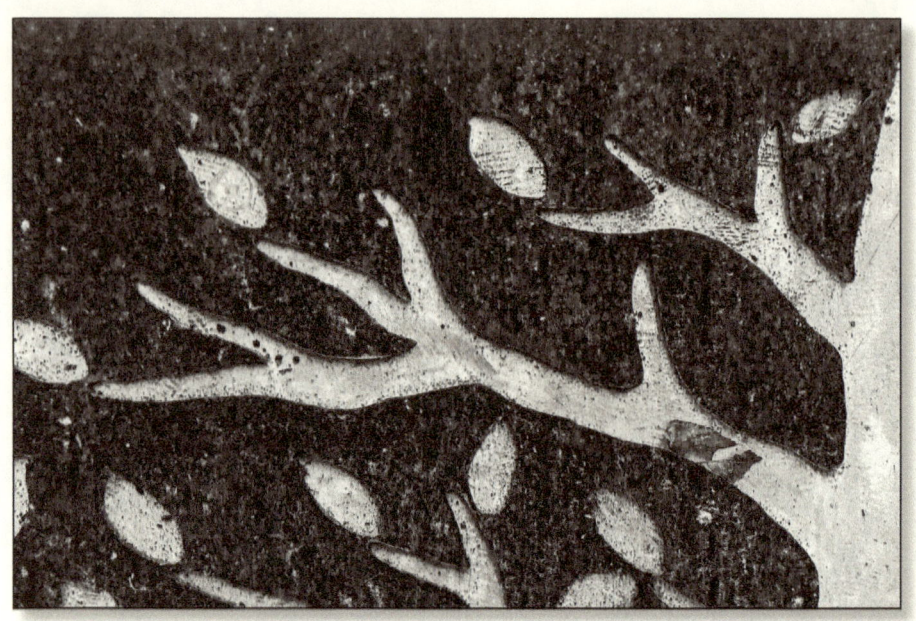

Skidmore, Saratoga Springs, N.Y., Nov. 22, 2014.
Nikon D7000, 28mm, 1/640, f/2.8, ISO 400, Tv, spot metering
Photo © 2014, 2015 by Shawn M. Tomlinson

consider moving to the next level of DSLR, which in this case, would be the Nikon D7000, D7100 or D7200.

In most cases, upgrading is not a good idea within the same camera class unless it has been a long time since your DSLR was made. So, yes, if you have a 3-megapixel Canon EOS D30 it makes sense to upgrade to a 20.2-megapixel Canon EOS 70D, and not just for the resolution increase. The D30 (not Canon's later 30D) was a great DSLR in its day in 2000, but it's probably not the best choice for your current main camera. Upgrading from a 40D to a 50D is less useful.

Upgrading makes more sense if you go to the next class up.

Going from entry level to enthusiast or enthusiast to semi-pro or semi-pro to pro DSLRs gets you some significant improvements.

The first, in each category, is better, tougher camera construction. Entry level DSLRs are cheaper because they are made cheaper. They are largely plastic and have fewer user controls. They are great for casual photographers only wanting good photos of the family and friends, and for use online. Moving to the enthusiast level gets you more metal in the camera and better controls. This continues up to

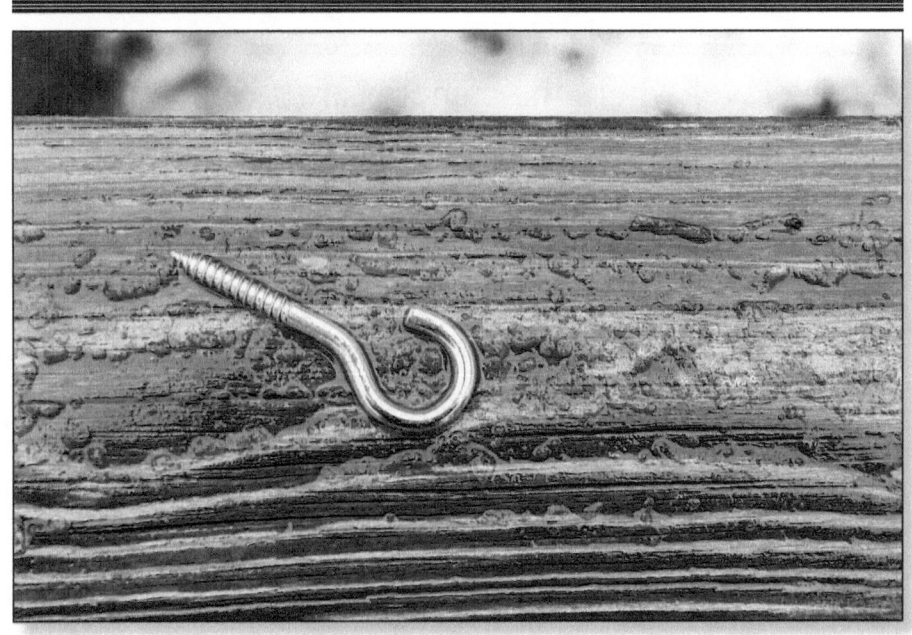

Ballston Lake, N.Y., Dec. 9, 2014.
Nikon D7000, 28mm, 1/200, f/2.8, ISO 400, Tv, spot metering
Photo © 2014, 2015 by Shawn M. Tomlinson

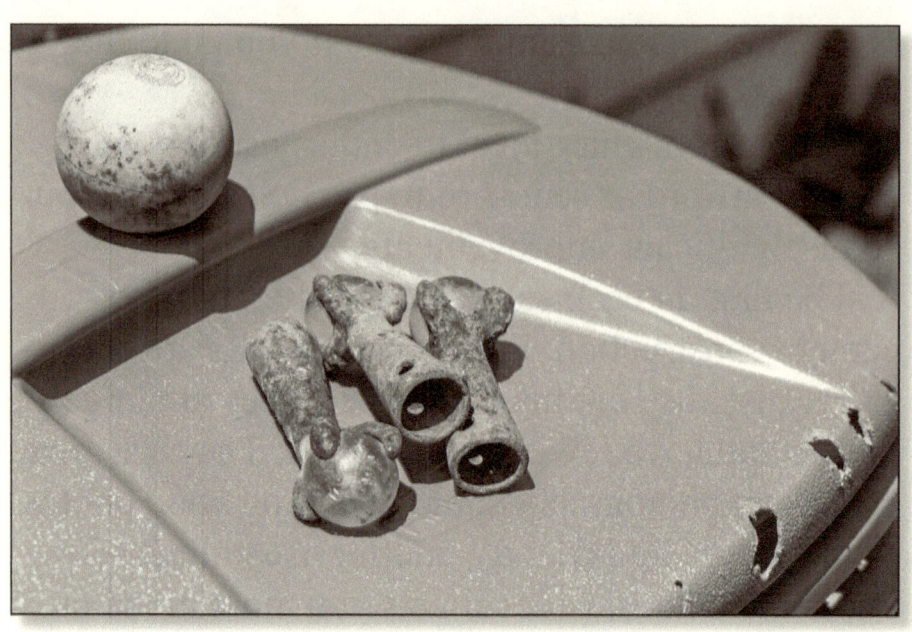

the pro level where the cameras are strong enough — almost — to be run over by a car. They are all magnesium alloy and weather-sealed, which means shooting in a hurricane is possible without ruining your camera.

Of course, the camera makers use better materials and components in each level of DSLR, too, which improves handling and picture quality. So, for example, my 2.65-megapixel Nikon D1 will take far better photos than a 3-megapixel Casio. It's even comparable to a 6.1-megapixel camera like the Nikon D70 or Canon EOS D60 (not 60D). It does not have the detail of more modern DSLRs, but considering it was made in 1999, it still is a hell of a camera. I stupidly dropped it the other day and it went on working as if nothing had happened.

Not everyone wants or can afford a pro DSLR, but that's OK. There are plenty of other levels of cameras that are great. There's definitely a difference, though, between each class.

For example, I use the Nikon D7000 "enthusiast" DSLR as my main camera and my friend and photographic colleague, Gary Ziroli, uses a Nikon D300 as his. We occasionally trade cameras just

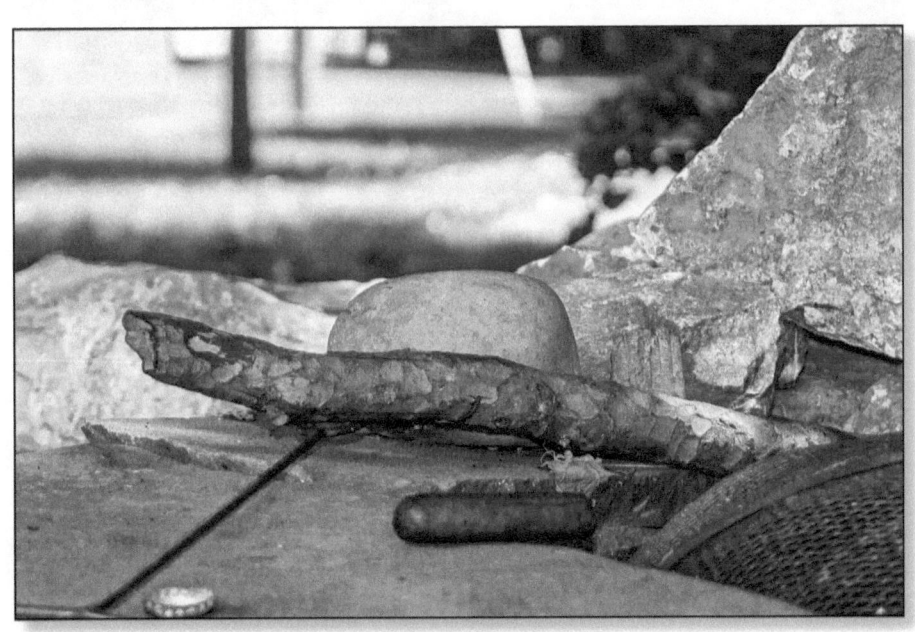

Clarksville, N.Y., June 8, 2014.
Canon EOS 20D, 80mm, 1/250, f/5.6, ISO 200, Tv, pattern metering
Photo © 2014, 2015 by Shawn M. Tomlinson

to experiment. I certainly prefer the image quality of the D7000 over the D300, although there isn't much of difference except for sharpness. The D7000 has 16.2 megapixels and the D300 has 12.2. I like a number of other things better about the D7000 than the D300, but the category in which the D300 beats the D7000 without question is build quality. Holding it, it feels much more solid and

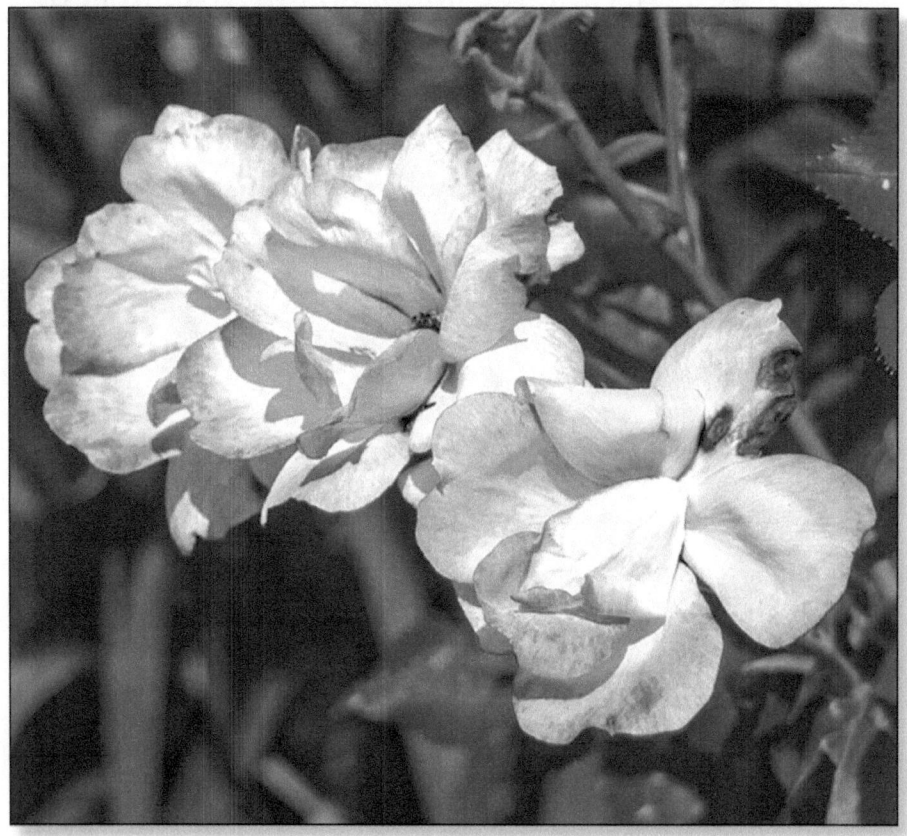

Saratoga Springs, N.Y., July 1, 2014.
Nikon D1, 75mm, 1/750, f/5.6, ISO 200, Av, pattern metering
Photo © 2014, 2015 by Shawn M. Tomlinson

substantial. It feels as though it can take much more of a beating than my camera.

We both tried a Nikon D3200 just to see if 24 megapixels would be worth it. There is a slight bit more sharpness and detail, but the flimsy construction of it put us both off. I also miss the top

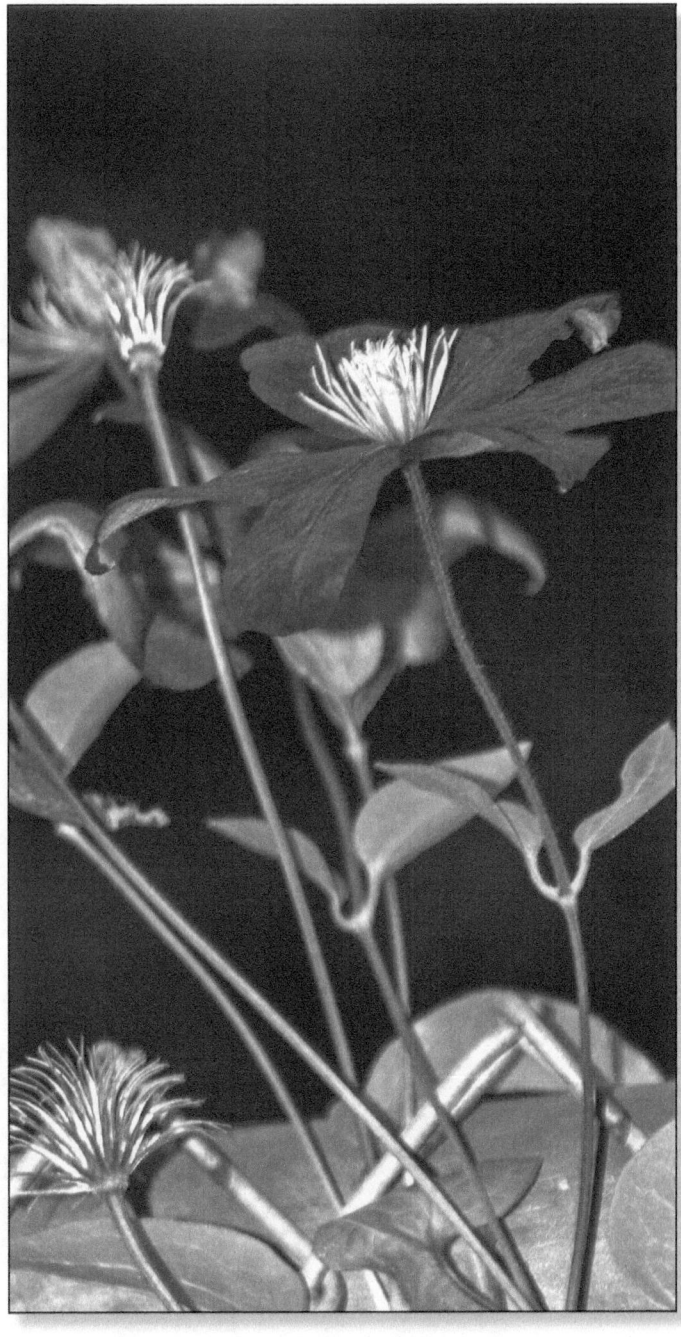

Saratoga Springs, N.Y., July 1, 2014.
Pentax K20D, 200mm, 1/180, f/6.7, ISO 140, P, pattern metering
Photo © 2014, 2015 by Shawn M. Tomlinson

right informational LCD.

What you consider important to you as a photographer is the main consideration in upgrading with a second DSLR.

3) Is it worth the money? This, again, is subjective. I would much rather put $1,000 into an older

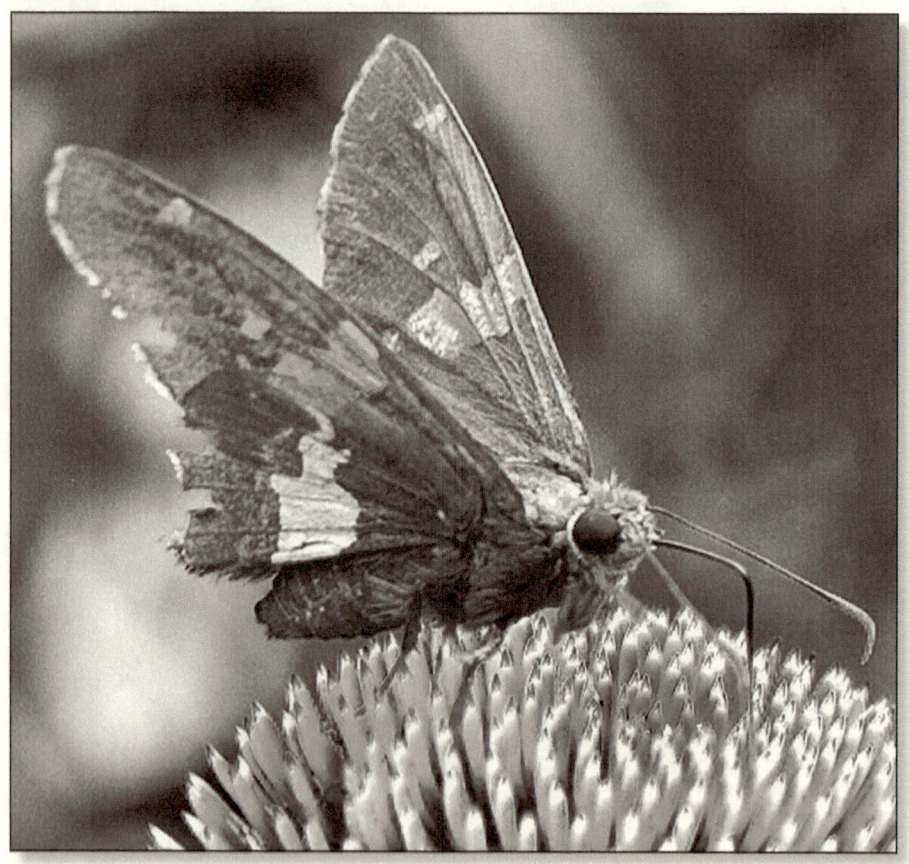

Saratoga Springs, N.Y., July 19, 2014.
Nikon D1, 55mm, 1/250, f/5.6, ISO 200, Av, pattern metering
Photo © 2014, 2015 by Shawn M. Tomlinson

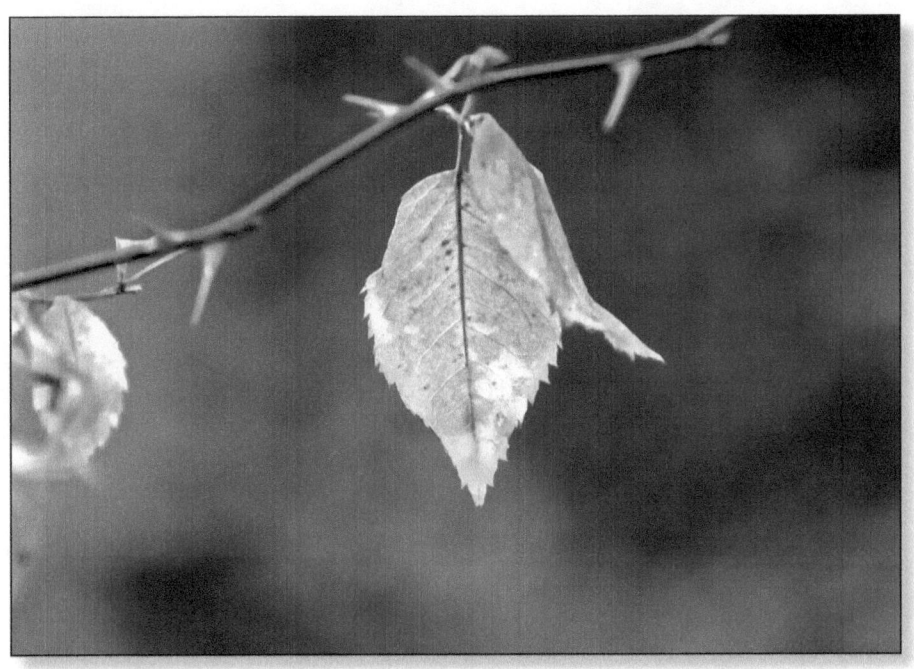

Ballston Lake, NY, April 9, 2015
Nikon D7000, 270mm, 1/640, f/5.3, ISO 800, S, pattern metering
© 2015 by Shawn M. Tomlinson

DSLR such as the full-frame Nikon D700 or Canon EOS 5D than the same money in a Canon EOS 7D. Full-frame is a better format with sharper images, even in older cameras.

You may feel differently. You may want to put the money into a newer DSLR because you like the features better and you already have lenses for the crop-frame APS-C type camera that may not work particularly well on full frame DSLRs.

4) Investing in better lenses always will make your images better than buying the newest spiffiest

DSLR. Put a top quality lens on your old Nikon D70 and it'll be like a new camera. The images you will get will be superior to shooting with a Nikon D3300 with a low-end lens, such as one made by third-party companies such as Sigma, Tamron and Tokina, and far superior to anything marketed as Quantaray.

Better lenses make images better.

Period.

Investing in a high-quality lens may not be as much fun as playing with a new DSLR, but the results in your images will show you quickly that the money was well spent.

When I put my Nikon AF D 28mm prime lens on my D70 or even my D1, the image quality goes up. There is more detail and the subjects are sharper.

There are other good reasons for getting a newer or second DSLR, but if you really want an increase in image quality, a better lens is the way to go.

Reason 2
Experimenting

That sparkling brand new DSLR you bought cost a lot of money. You take great care not to get it hurt. It stays in the gadget bag whenever you're not shooting.

And maybe you don't shoot as much as you would if you could use a DSLR that cost less.

Or, maybe, you'd just like to see how other DSLRs work and what kind of images they produce.

All these were true for me.

My first DSLR, the Pentax *ist DS did get a lot of use because I was shooting a lot for the newspaper where I was the Sunday editor. But when I upgraded to a second DSLR, the Pentax K20D, I was overly cautious in handling it. Unconsciously, I was coddling it. I know if I smashed it, it would be quite some time before I could replace it.

And, sure, I'd always wanted to try Nikon and Canon DSLRs, but they were more expensive than Pentax cameras. I had used the Nikon D1, D80 and D90 for the newspaper, but they weren't mine and I never really experimented with them.

Come to find out, older DSLRs — especially entry level and mid-range models — have fallen out of favor with many people because of their interesting in pursuing the megapixel chase.

Suddenly, entry level and mid-range DSLRs only a few years old are a fraction of the cost they originally were.

This gives you the chance to buy them cheap and experiment.

A new entry level DSLR costs anywhere up to $1,000, and a mid-range up to $2,000.

A used entry level DSLR can cost as low as $50 and a mid-range as low as $70.

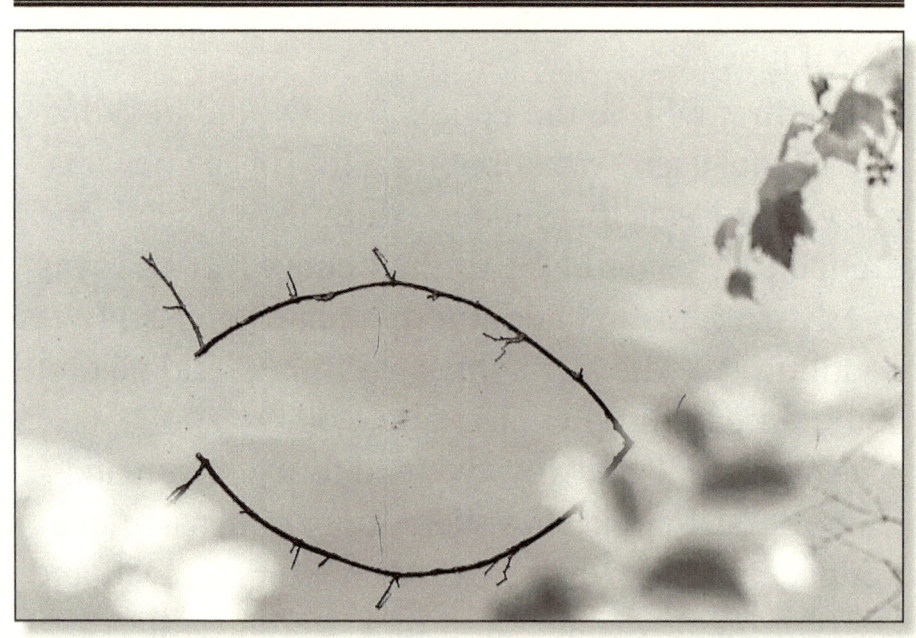

Mayfield, N.Y., Aug. 1, 2014.
Nikon D70, 180mm, 1/1250, f/4.8, ISO 200, Tv, pattern metering
Photo © 2014, 2015 by Shawn M. Tomlinson

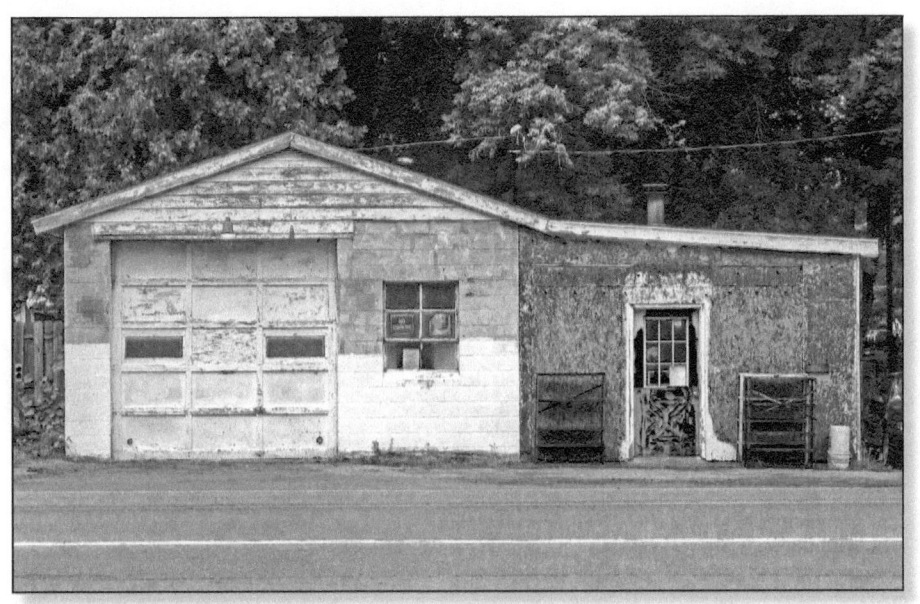

Ganesvoort, N.Y., Aug. 9, 2014.
Canon EOS 20D, 60mm, 1/2500, f/5, ISO 400, Tv, pattern metering
Photo © 2014, 2015 by Shawn M. Tomlinson

I got my chance.

With some birthday money to blow, I paid immediately for a Nikon D70 at $79. I already had a Nikon AF D 28-80mm lens from my Nikon F4S film SLR, so I was ready to go the moment it arrived. Immediately I tested it to see how it would do in low light, and it beat my much more expensive and newer Pentax K20D. Color-wise, just as good if not better.

I didn't stop there.

I invested another $69 in a Canon EOS 10D and $35 for a Canon EOS Rebel film SLR just because it had a Canon EF II 28-80mm lens attached to it.

The 10D produced the best color straight from the camera I'd ever seen.

Soon, the original DSLR, the Nikon D1 arrived and despite the 2.65-megapixel resolution and ancientness of this camera, it also had great color and produced wonderful images.

Buying these older DSLRs gives you a chance to try things without putting your

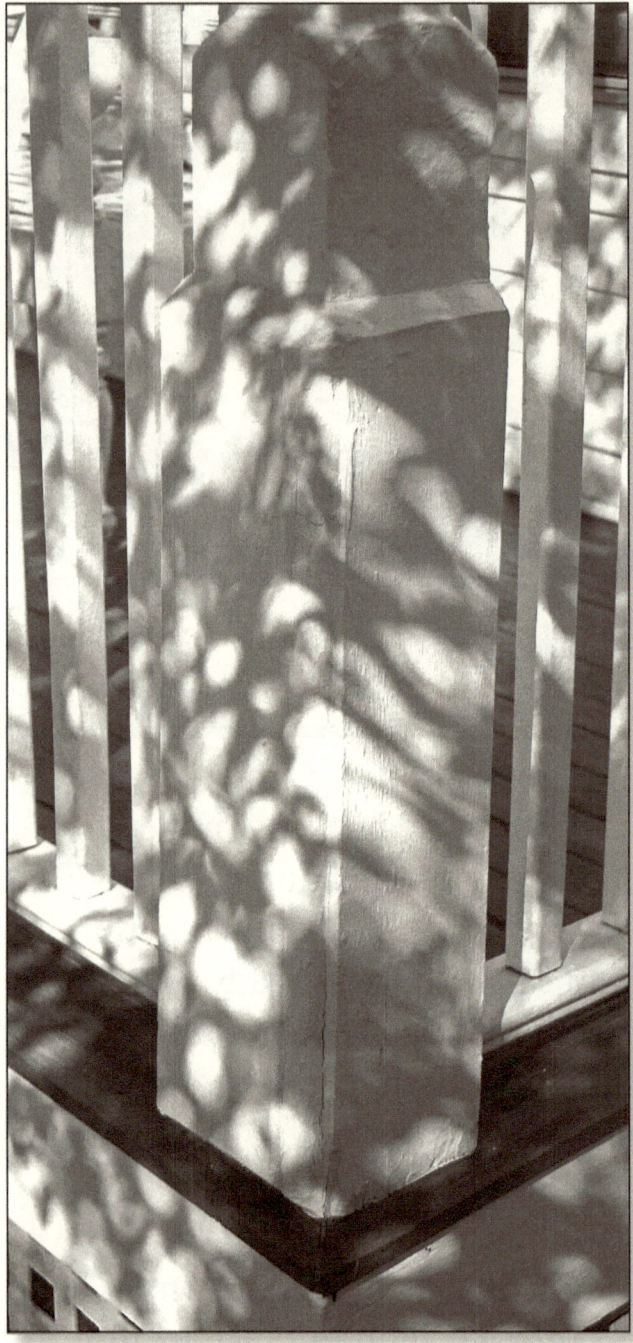

Saratoga Springs, N.Y., Aug. 19, 2014.
Canon EOS 20D, 35mm, 1/2500, f/3.5, ISO 400, Tv, pattern metering
Photo © 2014, 2015 by Shawn M. Tomlinson

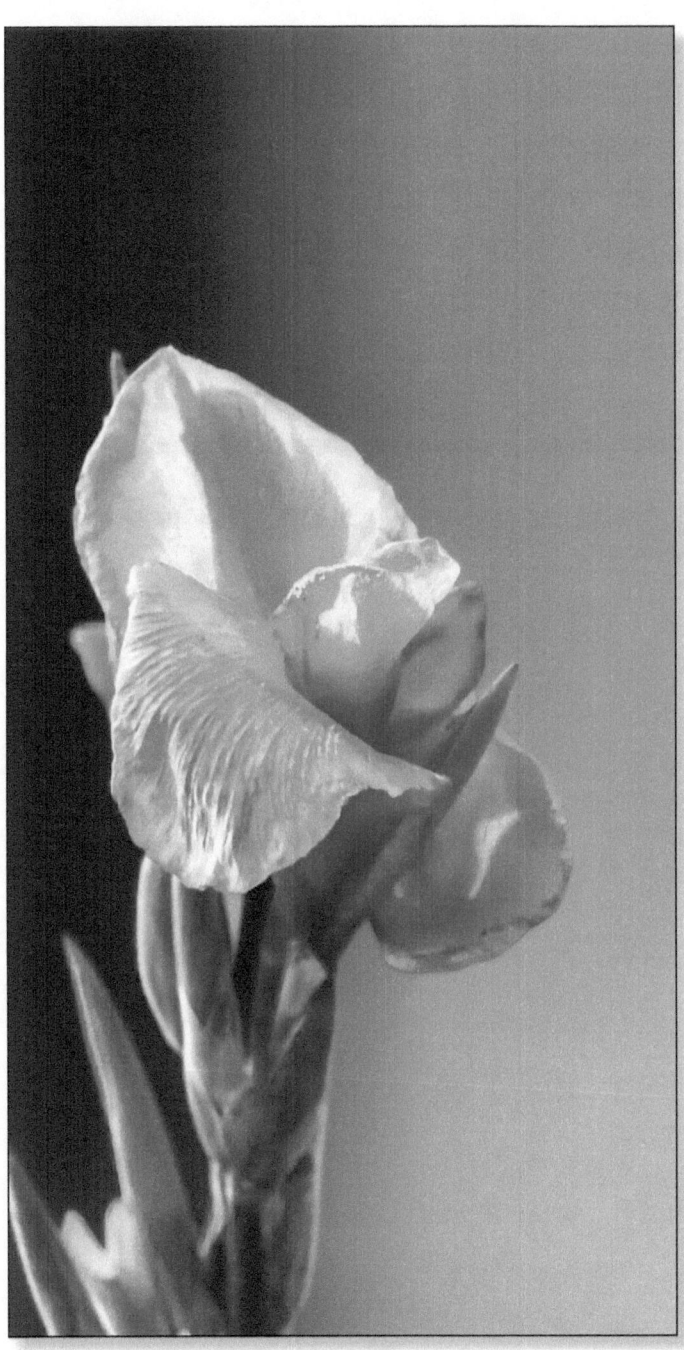

Clifton Park, N.Y., Aug. 19, 2014.
Nikon D70, 300mm, 1/800, f/6, ISO 400, Tv, pattern metering
Photo © 2014, 2015 by Shawn M. Tomlinson

main camera at risk, and they can bring a sense of fun to your photography.

They also can serve as tests to see if you have the right DSLR for you.

Let's say, for example, that you are a long-time Pentax user, even starting back in the film days. You've been fairly happy with your Pentax K10D, but you've been thinking about buying a new DSLR to use as your main camera, essentially replacing your K20D. You had been considering the Pentax K-5 IIs or even the Pentax K-3. Either of those cost quite a bit, so perhaps in the meantime, you want to find out how the other DSLRs are, the kinds of images they produce.

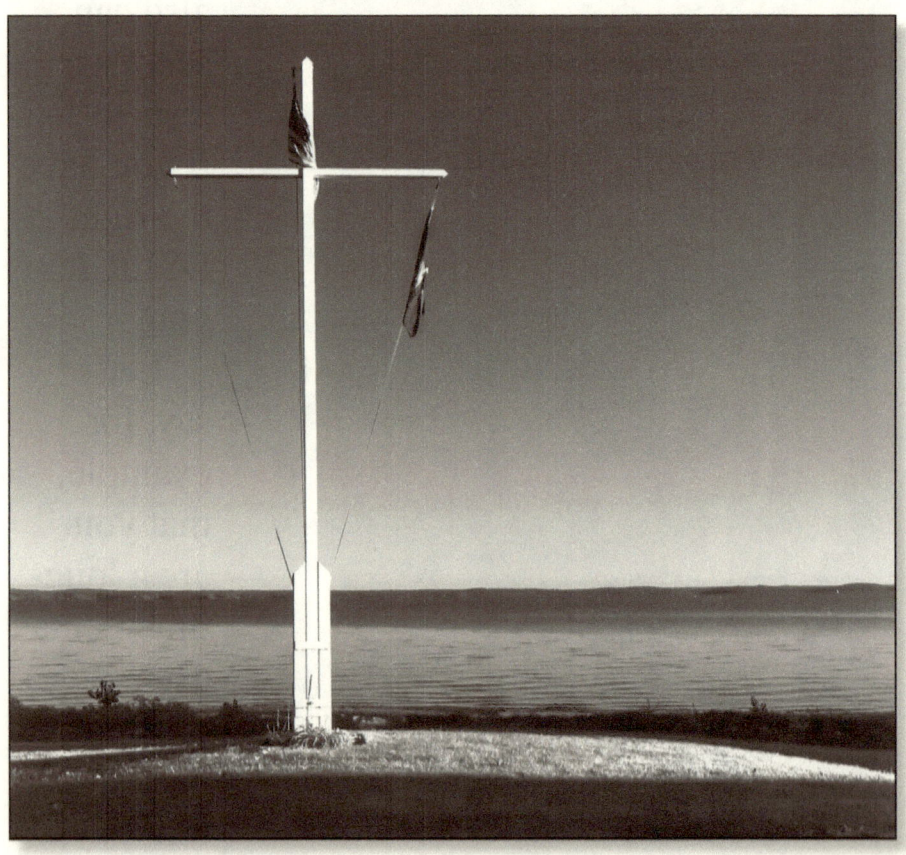

Great Sacandaga Lake, Mayfield, N.Y., Sept. 7, 2014.
Canon EOS 1Ds, 28mm, 1/320, f/11, ISO 250, P, pattern metering
Photo © 2014, 2015 by Shawn M. Tomlinson

So, you buy a Nikon D70 and a Canon EOS 20D. Even together and with lenses, these cameras will cost you about a third of a new Pentax, and you still plan to upgrade. This is just fun money.

Taking the D70 out, you find that it focuses much faster than your Pentax, and the colors seem richer. Shooting with the 20D also proves it has

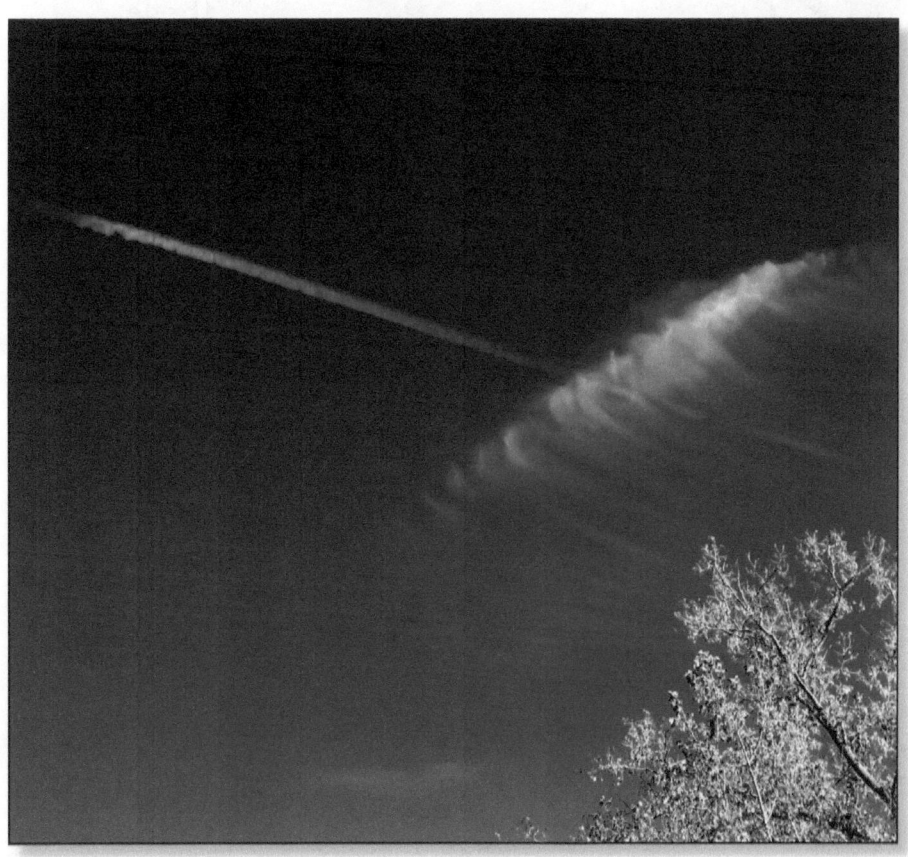

Indian Kill Nature Preserve, Glenville, N.Y., Sept. 28, 2014.
Nikon D7000, 32mm, 1/1600, f/5, ISO 250, Tv, center-weighted metering
Photo © 2014, 2015 by Shawn M. Tomlinson

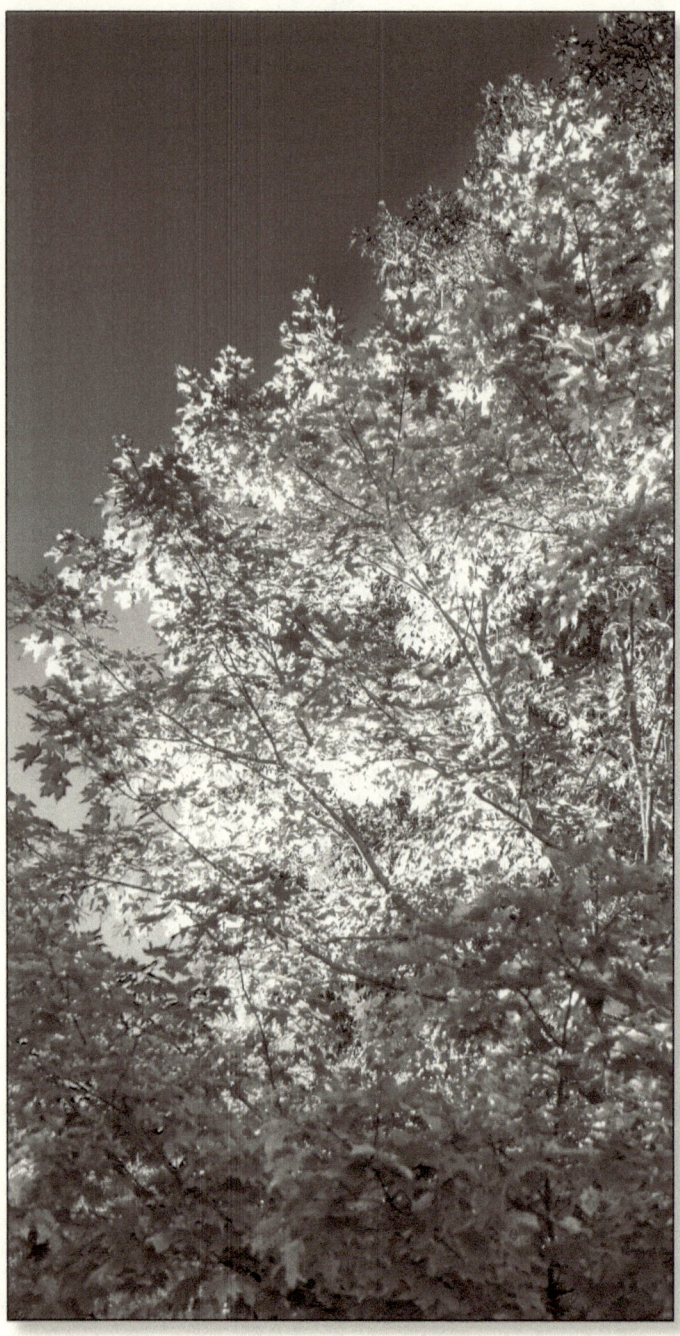

Indian Kill Nature Preserve, Glenville, N.Y., Sept. 28, 2014.
Nikon D7000, 18mm, 1/1600, f/3.5, ISO 250, Tv, center-weighted metering
Photo © 2014, 2015 by Shawn M. Tomlinson

faster fo-
cusing and
its colors
are much
warmer
than the
Pentax.
Even
though
these
are older
DSLRs,
they prove
to be better
in some
ways than
your main
camera.
Maybe
it's time to
think about
switching
brands.
This
happened
to me.
I had
been with

Pentax since 1982. I never thought I would switch.

It was the Canon EOS 10D, really, that made me think Canon might be the way to go for me. And it was, briefly. I invested in a full-frame Canon EOS 1DS, an older but better built — and full frame — DSLR than my Pentax

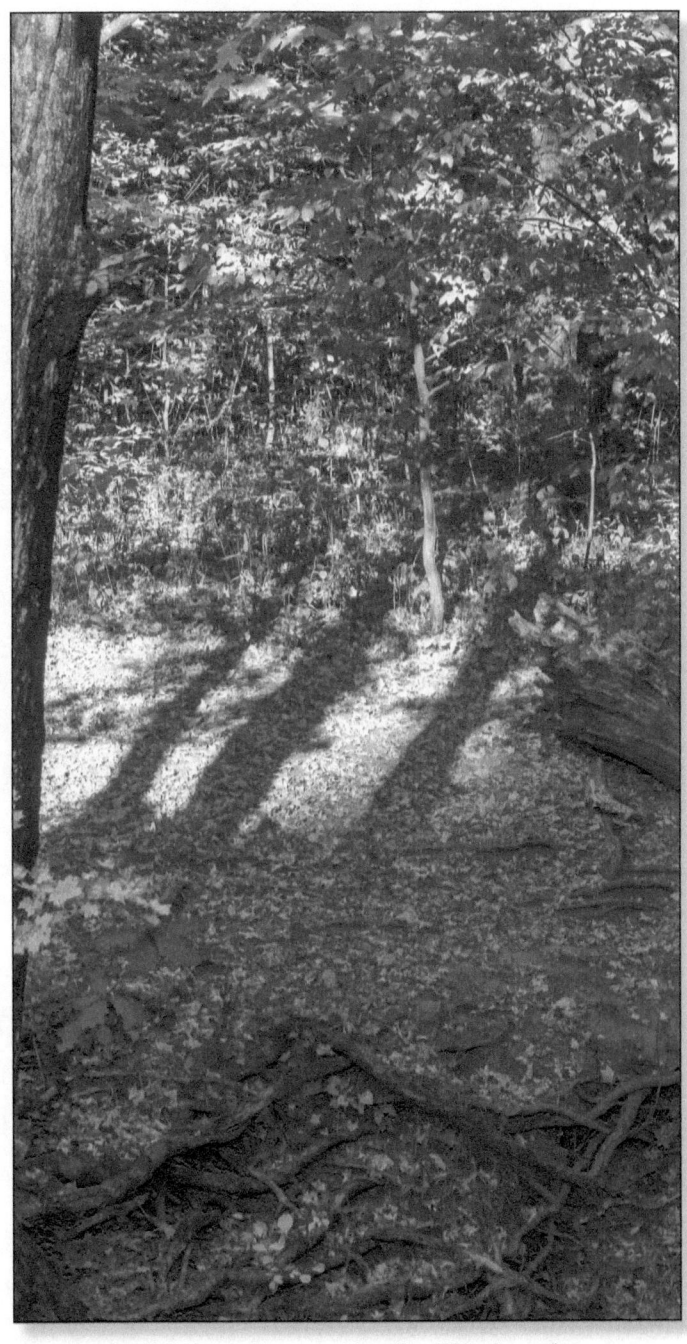

Indian Kill Nature Preserve, Glenville, N.Y., Sept. 28, 2014.
Nikon D7000, 55mm, 1/100, f/10, ISO 400, Tv, center-weighted metering
Photo © 2014, 2015 by Shawn M. Tomlinson

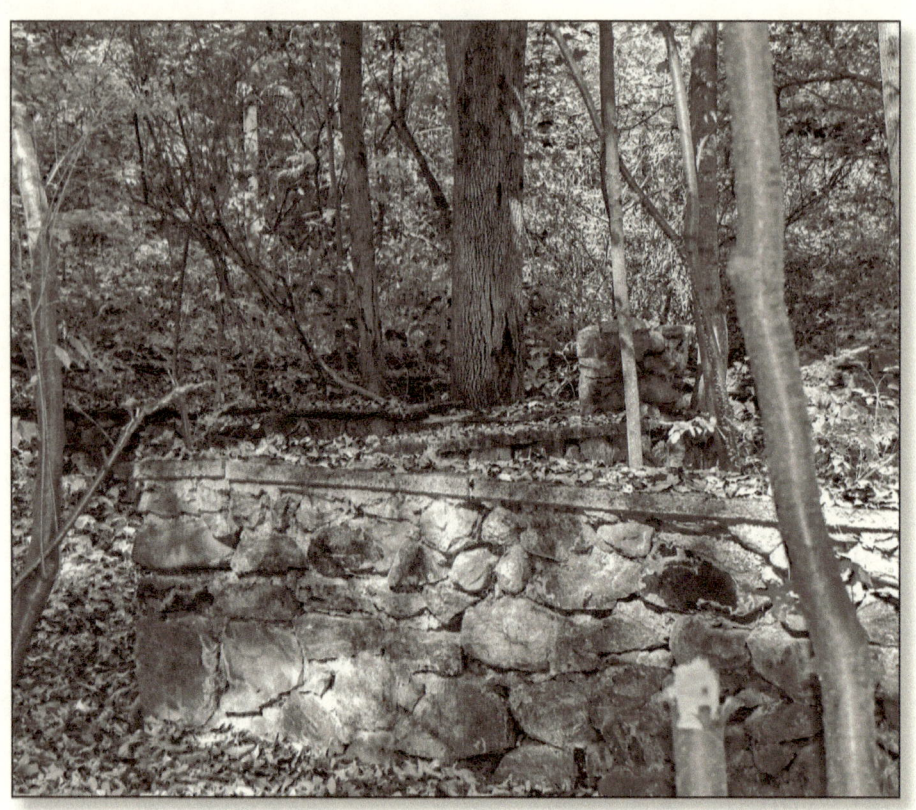

Robert W. Chambers estate, Broadalbin, N.Y., Oct. 3, 2014.
Nikon D7000, 31mm, 1/100, f/4.2, ISO 320, P, center-weighted metering
Photo © 2014, 2015 by Shawn M. Tomlinson

K20D. I'm sure I would have been happy with it, but buying used cameras does have some drawbacks. In this case, the sensor was developing problems and Canon said it was unfixable at this point.

So, I sent it back — one of the advantages of buying from a reputable used photo equipment dealer — and was hoping to replace it with the same model. The company didn't have another one,

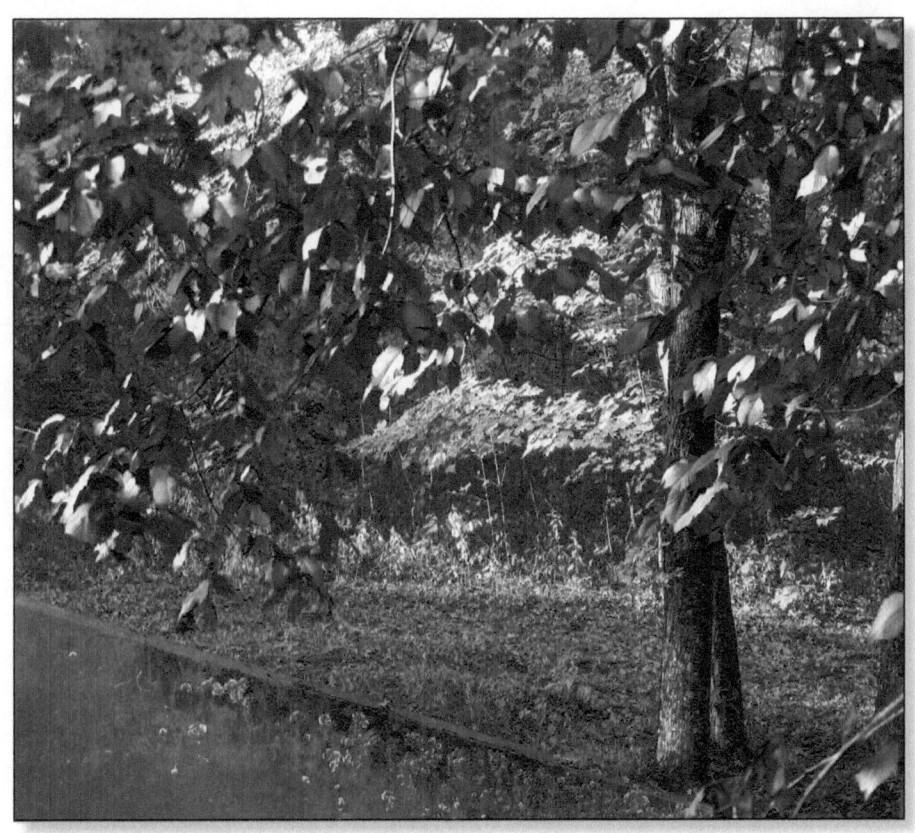

Indian Kill Nature Preserve, Glenville, N.Y., Sept. 28, 2014.
Nikon D7000, 55mm, 1/400, f/5.6, ISO 400, Tv, center-weighted metering
Photo © 2014, 2015 by Shawn M. Tomlinson

though, and my second choice, a Nikon D2x had just been sold. Almost reluctantly, I settled on a crop-frame DSLR, the Nikon D7000.

It turned out to be the best DSLR I've ever used. It's only a couple of megapixels higher in resolution than my K20D, but a couple of Nikon features — auto lens correction and Active-D Lighting — make all the difference. It's almost as though the

D7000 and K20D are in different camera classes, but they aren't. They were marketed to the same people and cost roughly the same when new. The K20D had a retail price in 2008 of about $1,200 and the D7000 had a list price of $1,100 in 2010.

I never would have known how good the D7000 is had I not taken the $79 chance on the D70.

But these older DSLRs aren't just throw-aways, either.

Don't let the lower megapixel count throw you.

All of the older DSLRs I have — including the ancient Nikon D1 — can produce fantastic images.

When I shoot with the D70 I may wish for just the tiniest bit more detail, but the photos still can be stunning.

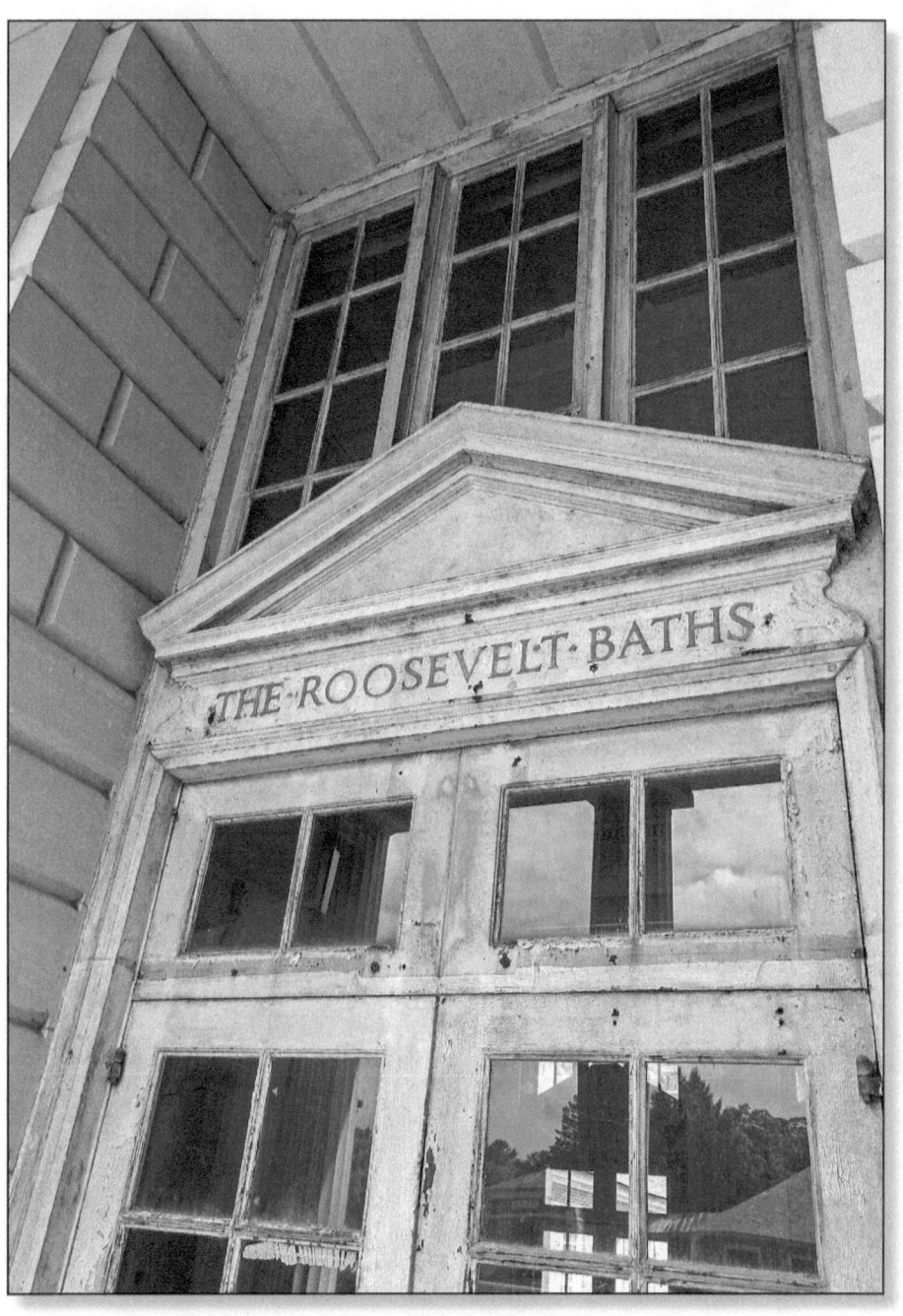

Roosevelt Baths, Saratoga Springs, NY, Aug. 2, 2014
Nikon D70, 18mm, 1/125, f/9, ISO 200, P, pattern metering
© 2014, 2015 by Shawn M. Tomlinson

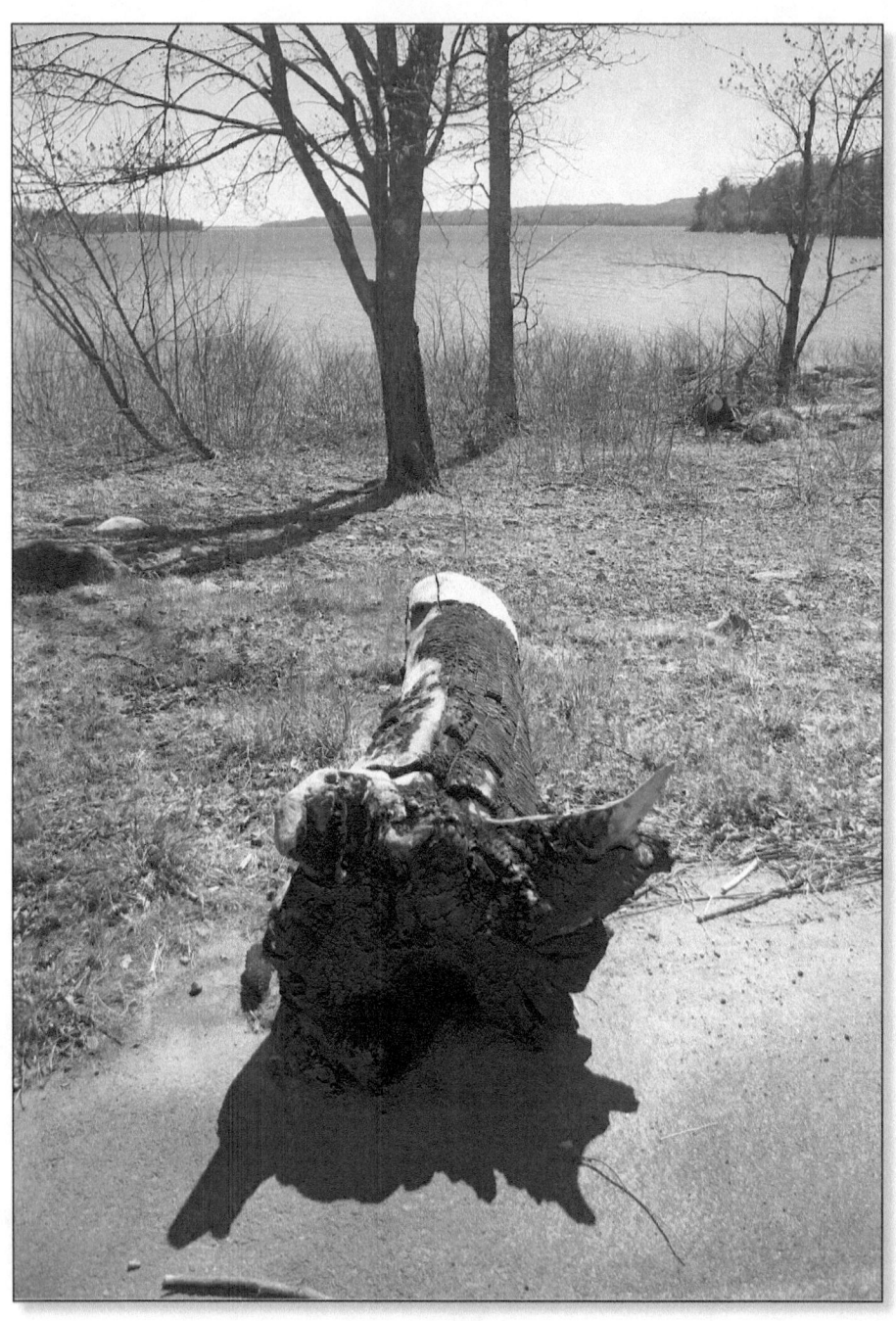

Boat Launch, Day, N.Y., May 3, 2013.
Pentax K20D, 18mm, 1/500, f/4.5, ISO 100, P, spot metering
Photo © 2013, 2015 by Shawn M. Tomlinson

Reason 3
Backup

Excitement reigns!

You just got your first paying photography job.

It's your Uncle Fred's wedding, and he's paying you because he's too cheap to hire a pro, but it's your first paying job, so ignore all that.

The big Saturday is here. You check to make certain the batteries are charged, the battery grip is functional and your Canon EOS 20D is working like clockwork. You have extra CF cards and an 18-200mm travel lens to make sure you get everything from the big picture to intimate closeups.

You're set.

Uncle Fred is just about to say "I do" when an "ERR99" message appears on the top right LCD of the 20D. You've read about ERR99. The DSLR has bought it. It's dead. No fix.

You're done shooting for the day and, under-standably, Uncle Fred and your new Aunt Bertha are a bit ticked.

What could you have done differently?

There's no way to predict the sensor or shutter seizing up and killing your camera. It can happen even on one much newer than the work-horse 20D.

You could how-ever, be ready for what my high school public speaking teacher called "the unpre-dictable predict-able." He said that in every pub-lic speak-ing (insert "photo-graphic") event, at least one unpredict-

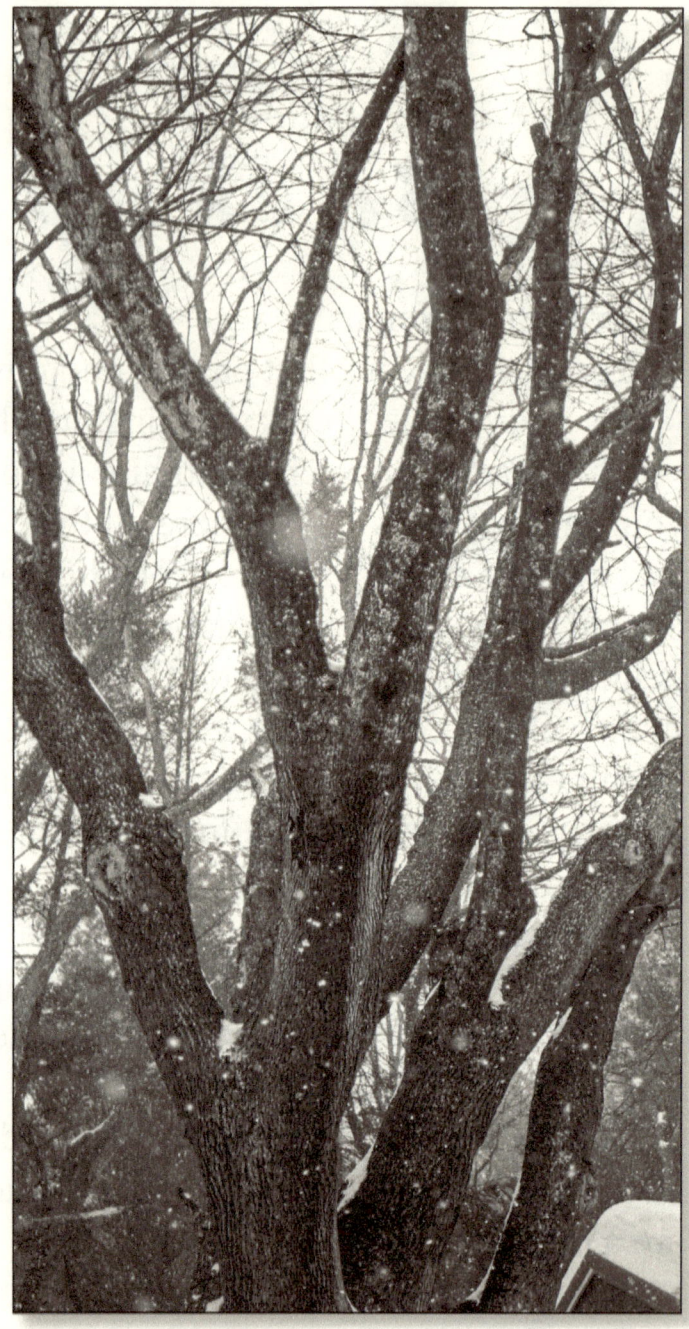

Broadalbin, NY, March 2, 2015
Nikon D2x, 28mm, 1/800, f/3, ISO 200, S, pattern metering
© 2015 by Shawn M. Tomlinson

able thing will happen. The key to surviving is to be prepared as well as possible for something you can't predict.

In this case, you needed a second DSLR camera body, something reliable and close in make and model to your main camera.

The least expensive solution for the Canon EOS 20D scenario above is having a second 20D in your gadget bag, also with battery grip and two charged batteries. A 20D camera body costs around $100, and that would have been a very cheap price to have paid to avoid Uncle Fred and Aunt Bertha telling the story of how you screwed up at every fami-

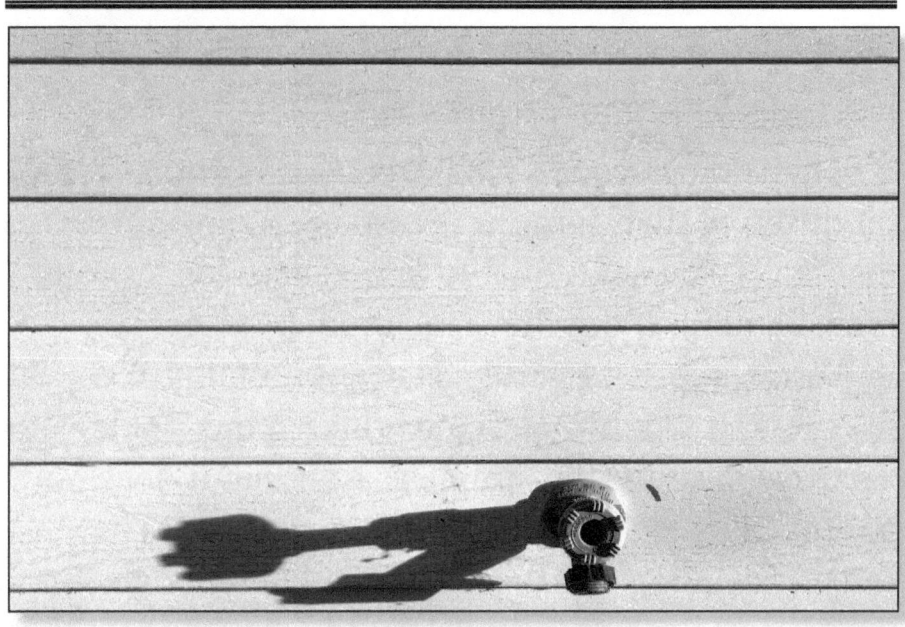

Ballston Lake, N.Y., Dec. 7, 2014.
Nikon D7000, 70mm, 1/640, f/5.6, ISO 400, Tv, spot metering
Photo © 2014, 2015 by Shawn M. Tomlinson

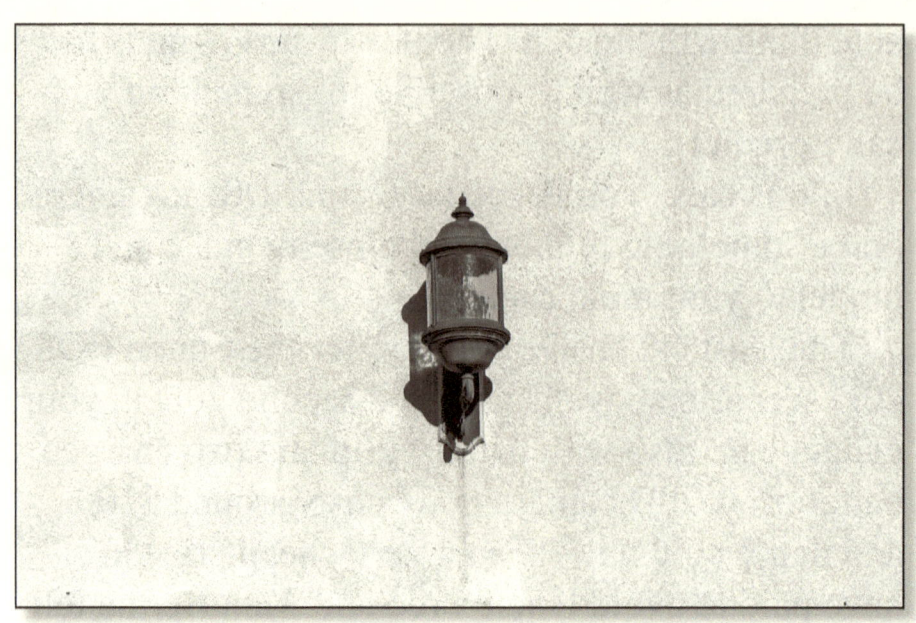

Saratoga Springs, N.Y., Dec. 20, 2014.
Nikon D70, 70mm, 1/1000, f/10, ISO 250, Tv, spot metering
Photo © 2014, 2015 by Shawn M. Tomlinson

ly gathering for the rest of time.

Choosing a second DSLR body as a backup is a bit different than for other reasons. You need one that is very close in quality and generation to your main camera, if not the same model.

For example, as good as a Canon EOS 10D DSLR is, it wouldn't have worked in the Uncle Fred scenario for the simple reason that it does not accept EF-S lenses such as the 18-200mm. The same for Canon's earlier D30 and D60 models. So, the earliest backup for you would have been a second 20D.

The reason you need one close to your main camera is for consistency of image quality.

A Nikon D70, as mentioned above, is a fantastic camera, but it isn't a great backup for a D7100. Aside from the D70's 6.1 megapixels vs. the D7100's 24 megapixels, the

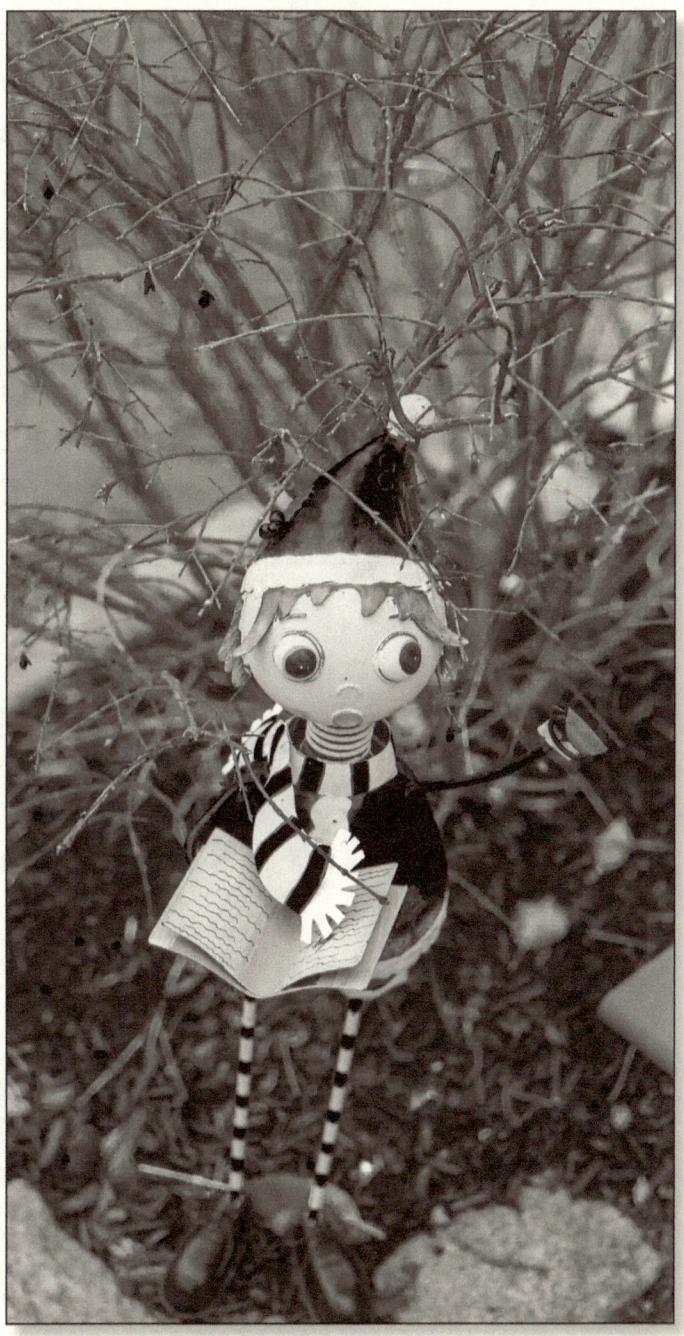

Saratoga Springs, N.Y., Dec. 26, 2014.
Nikon D300, 35mm, 1/1000, f/2.8, ISO 400, Tv, spot metering
Photo © 2014, 2015 by Shawn M. Tomlinson

latter has several features the D70 doesn't. Most notably these are Active-D Lighting and auto lens correction. The D7100 also handles low-light situations better than the D70, not only in focusing faster, but also it has much less red-green-blue (RGB) noise in dark areas. Although megapixels do not mean as much as most people think, there is a difference, and this will be much more noticeable in photos shot under the same circumstances.

Shooting the vows at the altar with the D7100

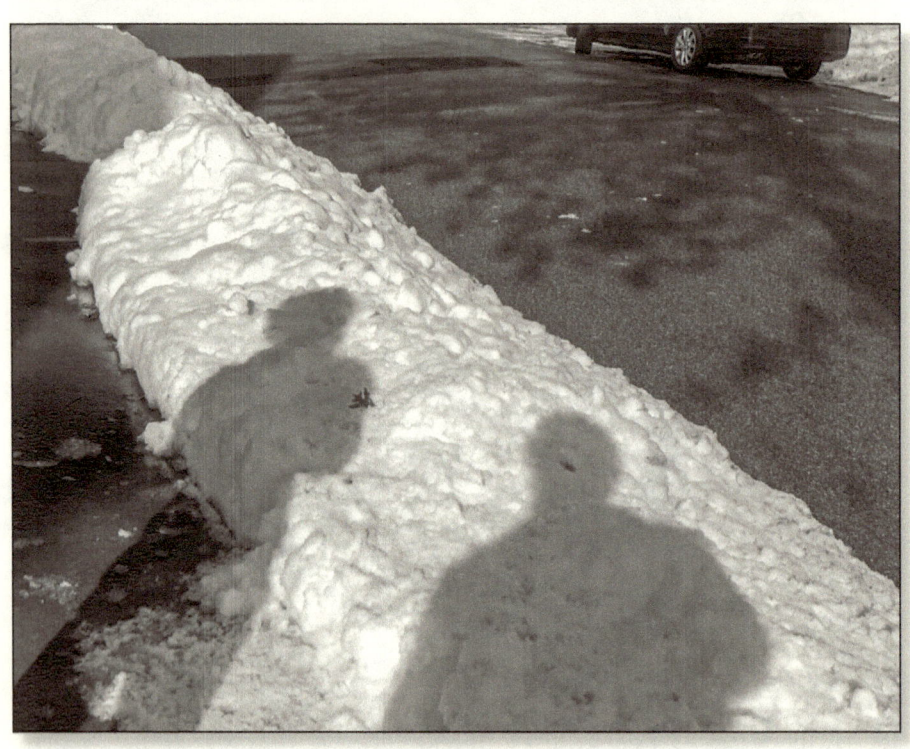

Gary Ziroli, Shawn Tomlinson, Saratoga Springs, N.Y., Dec. 13, 2014.
Nikon D1, 28mm, 1/1500, f/5.6, ISO 200, Av, pattern metering
Photo © 2014, 2015 by Shawn M. Tomlinson

and continuing after a failure of equipment with the D70 will make the images look quite different, especially with the aforementioned noise levels. This difference is far smaller when shooting in good, bright sunlight.

Choosing a backup DSLR as your second camera takes a little thought, but in general, it should not be more than one generation back and it should be in the same DSLR class if possible. Or it should be the same model.

For example, if your main camera is the Canon EOS 5D Mark III, the backup should be the Canon EOS 5D Mark II; if you shoot mostly with the Nikon D7100, the D7000 should be your backup.

One other idea, though, is worth considering with one stipulation.

Let's say you shoot with the D7000. It has 16.2 megapixels and sits roughly in the middle of Nikon's lineup if you remove the super-megapixel D810. It's a fantastic camera, but a lot of the quality of the images depends upon the quality of the lenses you use. Putting that 18-200mm lens on the D7000 will give you a lot of flexibility, but not the best image quality. If, however, you use a 50mm f/1.4 lens on it, your images will be stunning, but you will need to move around a lot to get the shots you want.

If you invest in a really good lens — one with

an "L" and a red line around it for Canon or one that says "FX" on it for Nikon — your images always will be better than with a cheaper lens on a better camera.

So the last alternative for a backup DSLR is a cheap, low-end, entry level camera such as the Nikon D3200 or

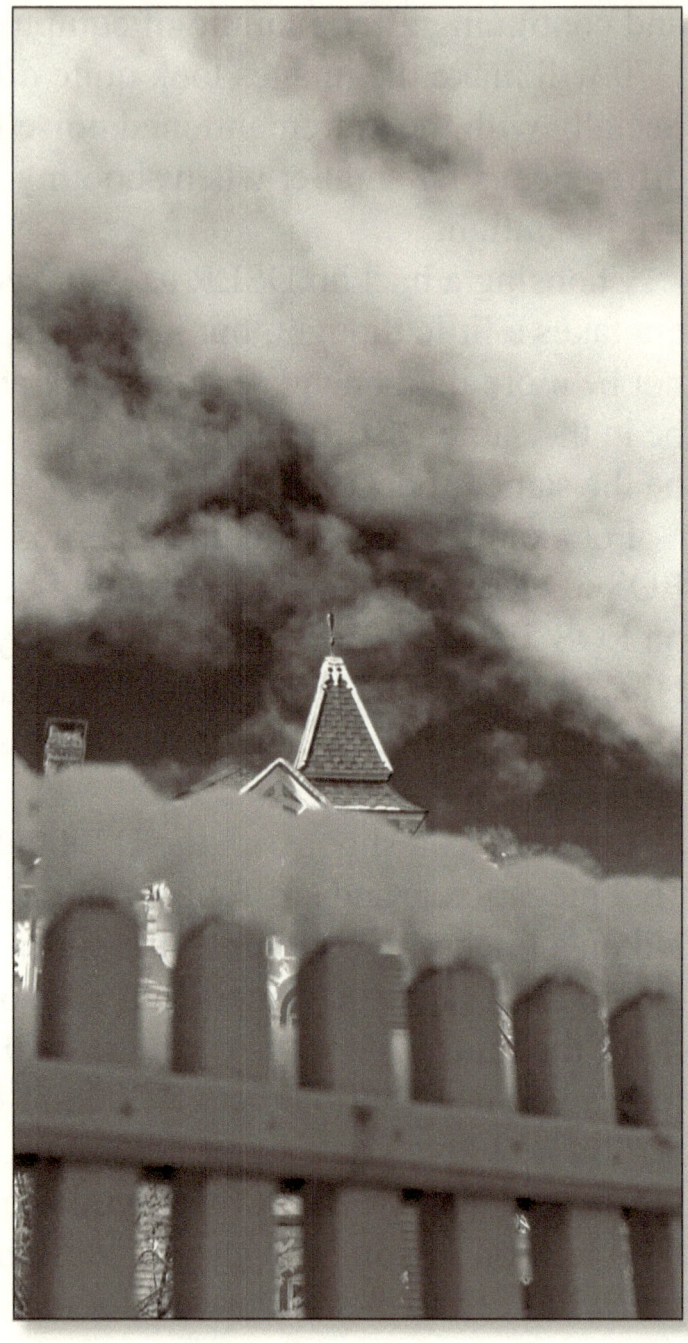

Saratoga Springs, N.Y., Dec. 13, 2014.
Nikon D1, 28mm, 1/800, f/5.6, ISO 200, Av, pattern metering
Photo © 2014, 2015 by Shawn M. Tomlinson

D3300.

This contradicts what I said about keeping the cameras close in model, but here's the reason this will work.

The D7000 has 16.2 megapixels and a 50mm f/1.4 lens, and this produces great photos. The D3200 has 24 megapixels and usually comes with a "kit" 18-55mm f/3.5-5.6 lens that's OK, but not the best. It will work very well as a backup DSLR, however — if you can get past the cheap plastic-ness of it — if you put that 50mm f/1.4 lens on it. Suddenly, you actually will be taking advantage of the D3200's high resolution, which most people don't because they don't invest in good lenses.

Using an entry-level DSLR as a backup, second camera has its drawbacks — chief among them that the controls are severely limited; take a lot of time to practice with it before an important photo session — but with the right lens, it will work.

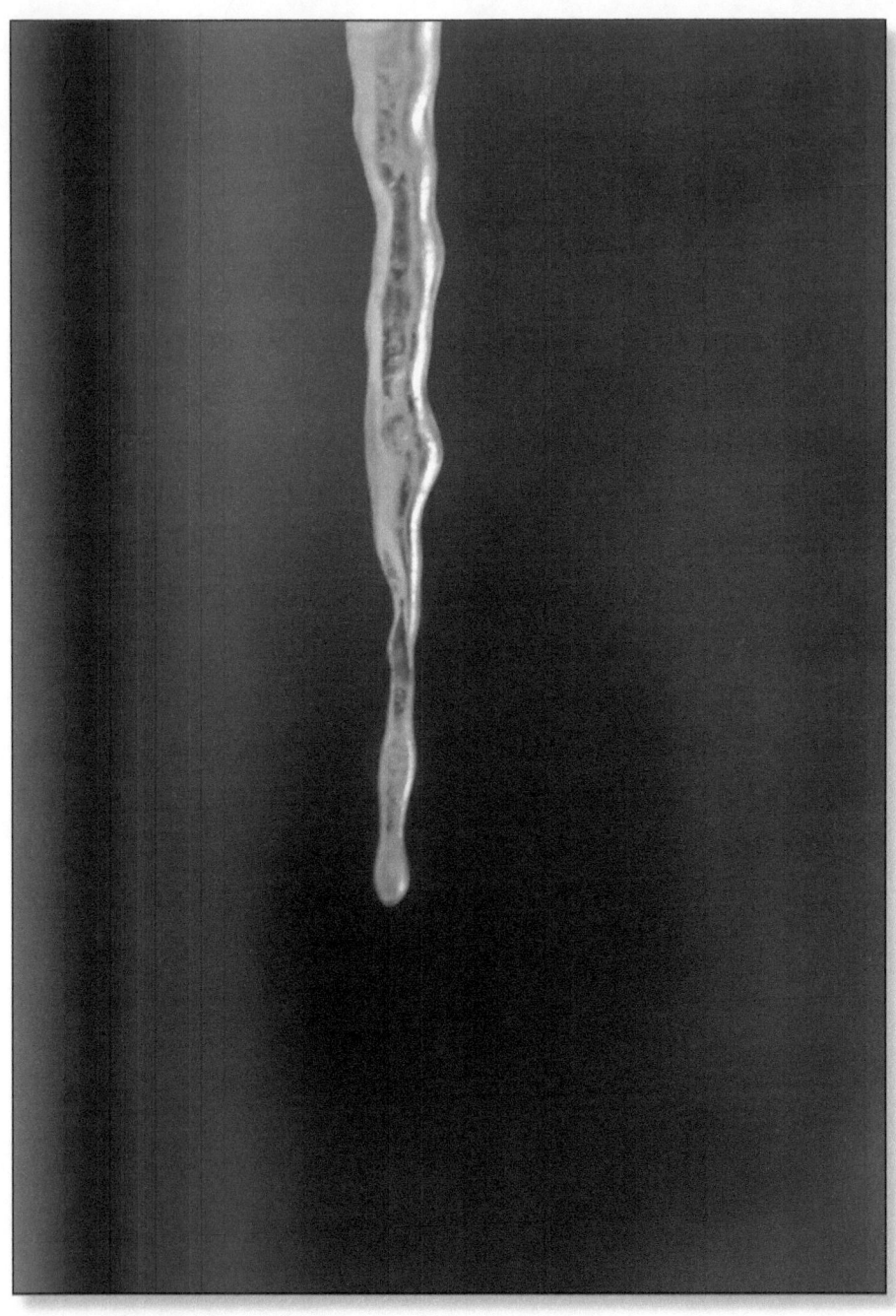

Ballston Lake, NY, March 5, 2015
Nikon D2x, 300mm, 1/320, f/5.6, ISO 400, S, pattern metering
© 2015 by Shawn M. Tomlinson

Reason 4
You're a Pro

Of course, if you're a professional photographer — meaning you make 90 percent or more of your living from photography — you probably already know the value of adding additional DSLR bodies, and you probably aren't reading this.

In case you are, the same things apply for you as for the weekend warrior photographer above. You cannot risk a DSLR camera failure during a shoot. Not only does it screw up that particular shoot, but it also can cause you problems getting future jobs. Word gets around, and no matter how good you are, people paying money for photographic work want someone truly reliable to hire.

Not all pros use pro DSLRs. The "big guns," the Nikon D4S and the Canon EOS 1DX are big money and for specific kinds of pros. Usually, photographers shooting sports or rapid-fire news events use these types of DSLRs. The cameras are tough and take a beating. That's a major concern for newspaper, wire and magazine photographers. They're in a hurry and can't be worried about banging their cameras against walls or airport ramps.

Pro DSLRs are big and heavy. There's nothing else quite like shooting with them, but not everyone needs them, including the pros. Professional photographers who are in less frantic situations routinely are moving more toward the semi-pro cameras such as the Nikon D610 or D810, or the Canon EOS 5D Mark III or even the Canon EOS 7D Mark II. These cameras are not as well built and not as heavy as pro DSLRs, but they produce top-quality images.

Even if you use a pro DSLR as your main camera, one of these DSLRs would be great choices for second camera bodies.

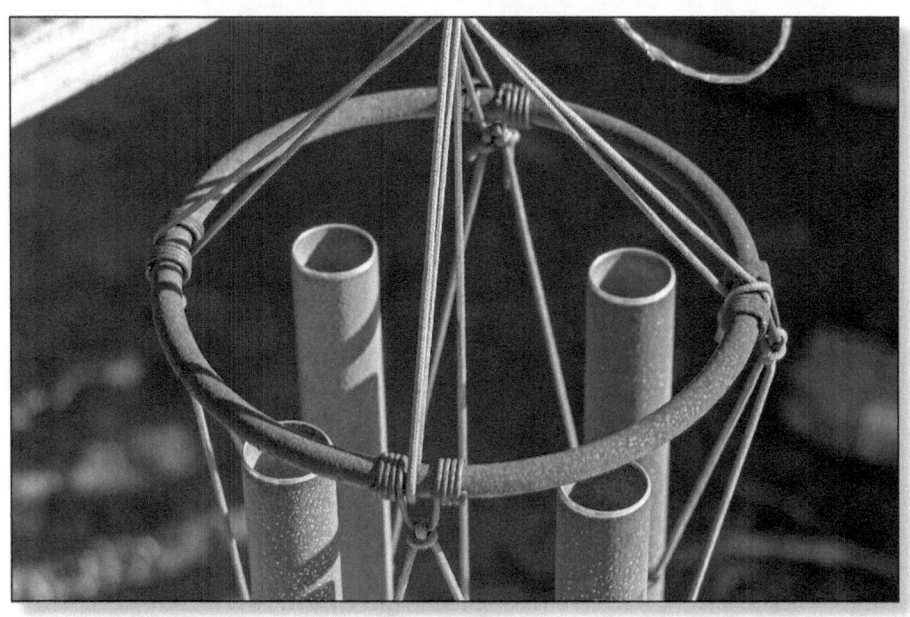

Ballston Lake, N.Y., Feb. 4, 2014.
Nikon D70, 80mm, 1/200, f/7.1, ISO 200, P, pattern metering
Photo © 2014, 2015 by Shawn M. Tomlinson

One thing that always annoys me is the snob feature of not having a popup fill flash on pro DSLRs. I don't use the fill flash much, and pros typically use major flash units on or off camera when they use flash at all. Still, I can't see the harm of putting a popup flash on a pro or semi-pro DSLR, even if you only use it once every 5,000 shots.

Oh well. Neither Nikon nor Canon has asked my opinion about this, and most pros don't seem to care.

When you do choose a second — and third and fourth — DSLR body for your professional work, remember that your professional reputation relies

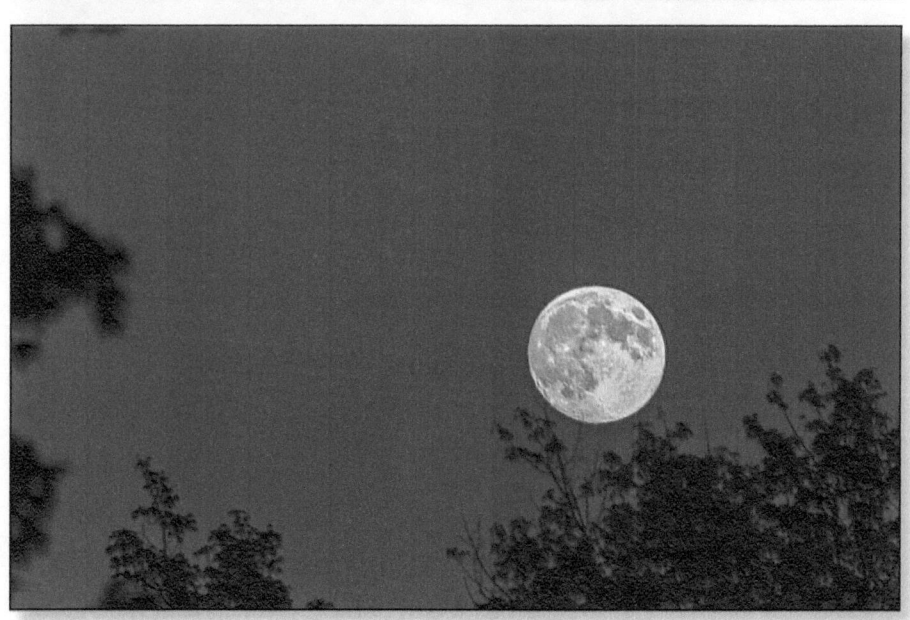

Ballston Lake, N.Y., Sept. 7, 2014.
Nikon D70, 300mm, 1/125, f/6, ISO 400, Av, pattern metering
Photo © 2014, 2015 by Shawn M. Tomlinson

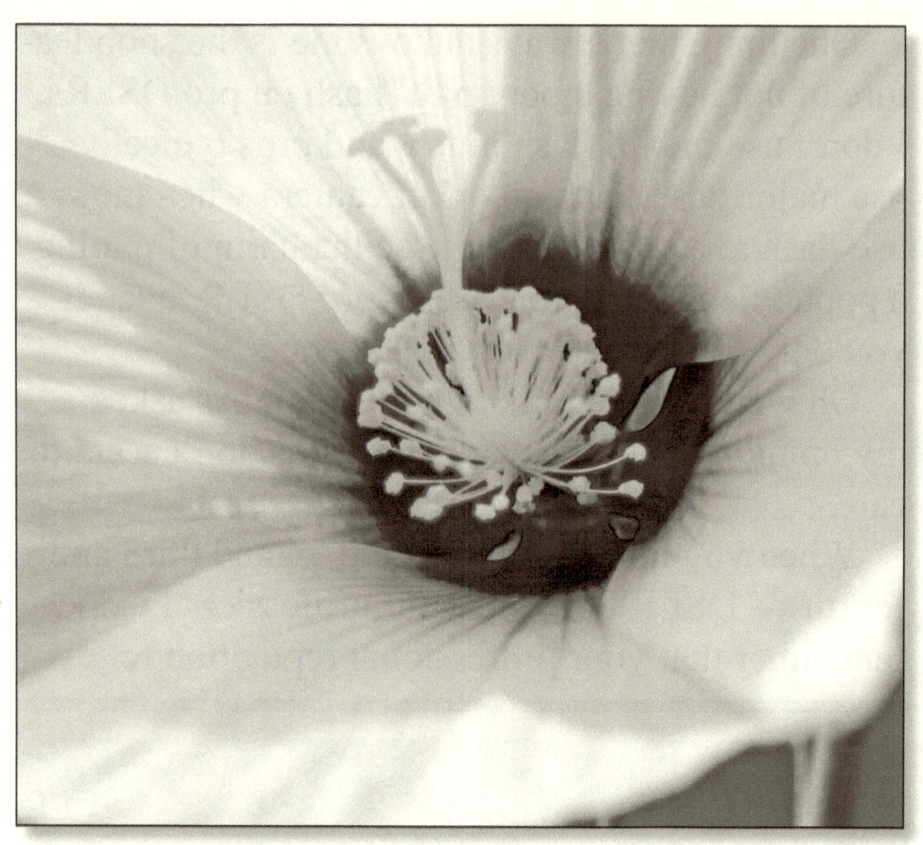

Saratoga Springs, N.Y., Aug. 5, 2014.
Nikon D1, 300mm, 1/1250, f/5.6, ISO 200, Tv, pattern metering
Photo © 2014, 2015 by Shawn M. Tomlinson

upon your choices. Unless I was desperate, I'd never shoot a pro job with the Nikon D70 or Pentax *ist DS, for example, despite how great these older cameras are. I might use the Canon EOS 20D because it is just that much better, but still borderline. The one thing that would sway me toward the 20D is that it shoots really fast. It shoots at 5 frames per second and has a reasonably good buffer, so it doesn't slow me down. Still... a camera closer to my main camera has advantages.

When I shoot, I want my backup to be nearly or as good as my main camera.

Clients rarely know anything about the equipment, but they want to see the professional results they paid for, and that means the best DSLRs I have at my disposal.

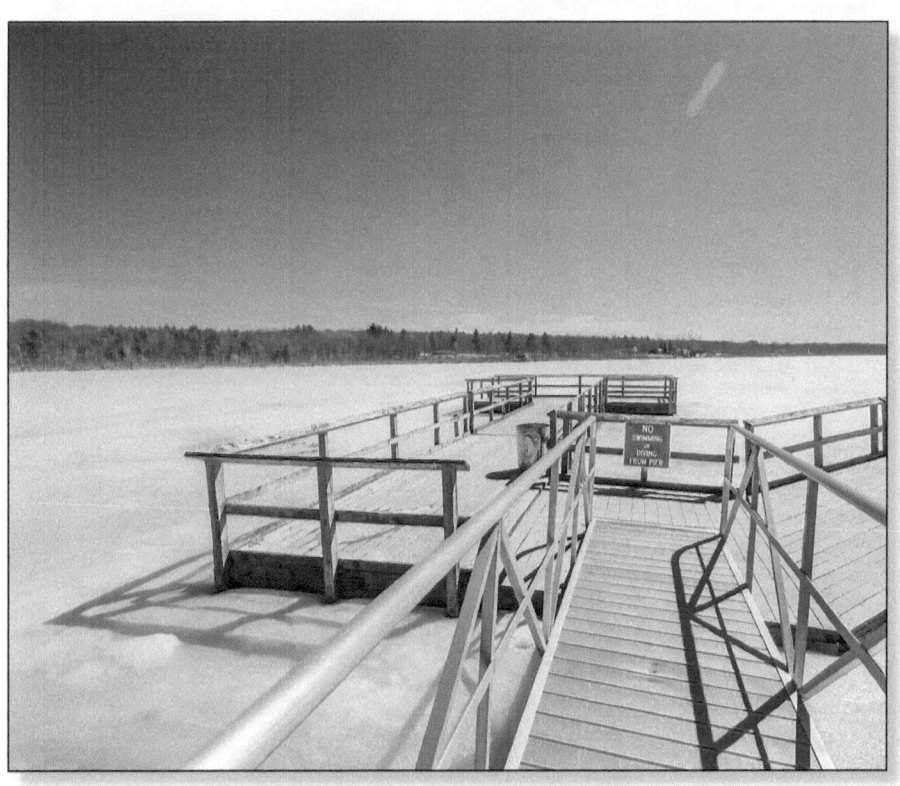

The lake, Ballston Lake, NY, April 1, 2015
Nikon D7000, 10mm, 1/1000, f/8, ISO 200, S, pattern metering
© 2015 by Shawn M. Tomlinson

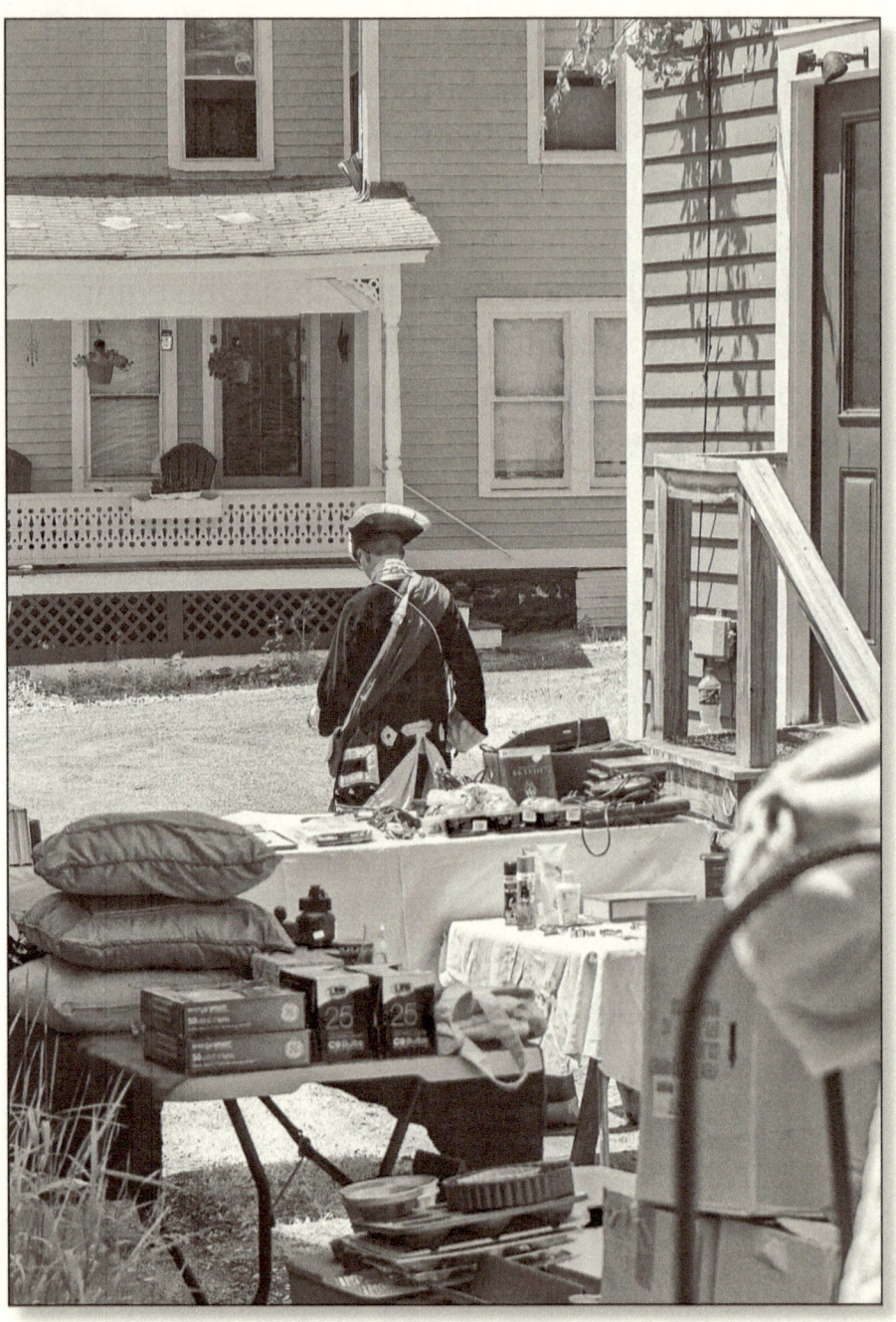

Revolutionary re-enactor, Greenwich, NY, June 20, 2015
Nikon D7000, 35mm, 1/1600, f/5, ISO 320, S, pattern metering
© 2015 by Shawn M. Tomlinson

Last Words

Some things I did not mention seem obvious, but I probably should state them anyway.

For example, unless you are buying a second DSLR to experiment, you probably want to

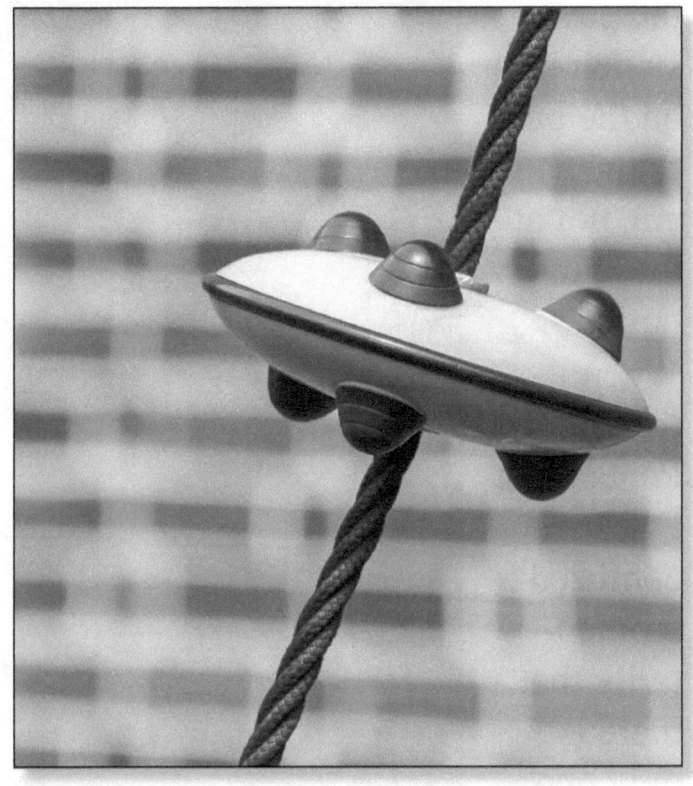

Saratoga Springs, N.Y., Aug. 5, 2014.
Nikon D1, 300mm, 1/1250, f/5.6, ISO 200, Tv, pattern metering
Photo © 2014, 2015 by Shawn M. Tomlinson

stick with the camera brand you already use.

The two main reasons for this are that it means you can use the lenses you already own on both cameras, and you already are familiar with the controls of the brand. I shoot with Nikons most of the time these days, so when I pick up the Canon EOS

20D, I immediately forget that the power switch is on the back of the camera, not at the shutter button. When I pick up the Pentax *ist DS, I am confused momentarily that there is only one command dial, not two, and there's that Fn (function) button on the back for things like shoot-

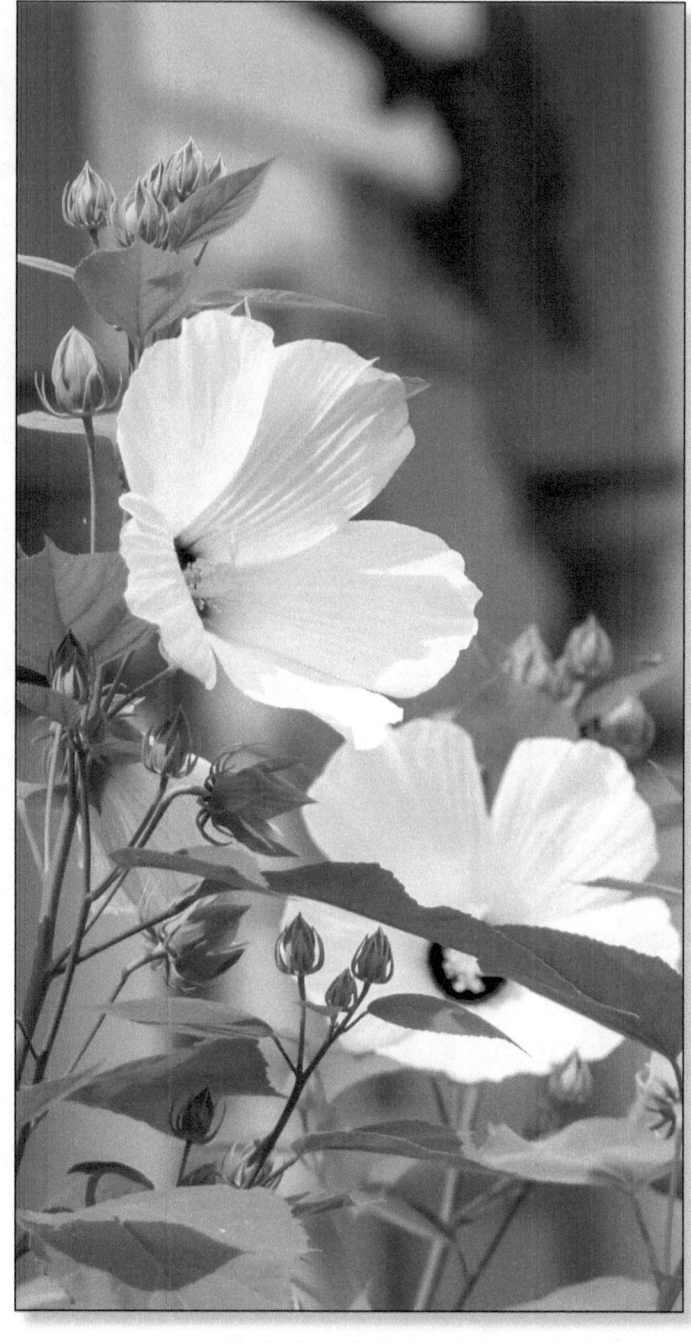

Saratoga Springs, N.Y., Aug. 5, 2014.
Nikon D1, 300mm, 1/1250, f/5.6, ISO 200, Tv, pattern metering
Photo © 2014, 2015 by Shawn M. Tomlinson

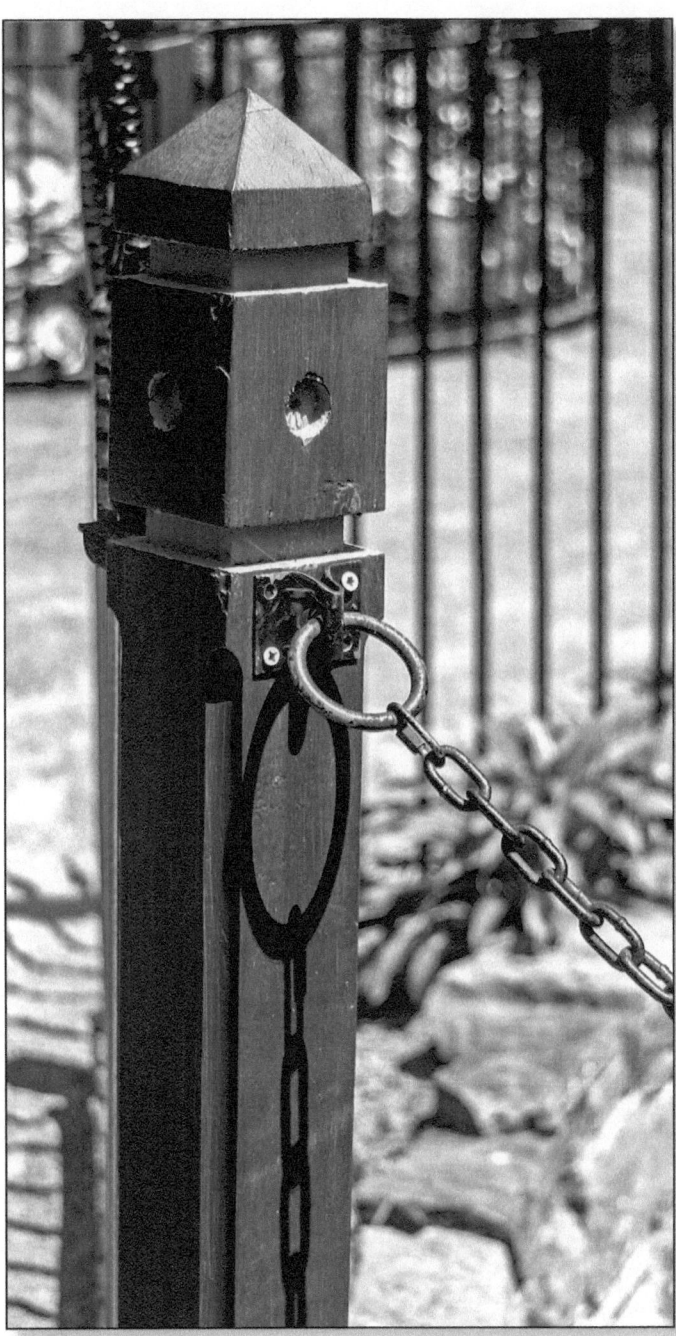

Congress Park, Saratoga Springs, N.Y., July 1, 2014.
Nikon D1, 62mm, 1/1000, f/5, ISO 200, Av, pattern metering
Photo © 2014, 2015 by Shawn M. Tomlinson

ing speed, white balance and ISO settings.

If you are upgrading or need a backup camera, you probably have a couple of lenses for your first DSLR, so why spend the extra money to start all over again by replacing those lenses?

You may want to buy better lenses — and

you should — but, again, those will work on both bodies.

By the nature of experimenting with different brands of cameras, you will need lenses — at least one per brand — that works on the new brand of camera but not on the old one.

A very inexpensive way to do this is to look on eBay or Goodwill for old film autofocus cameras that come with lenses. Few people want these old — and usually mostly plastic — cameras and their associated lenses, so they are not bid up often. The drawback is that you will not get really wide-angle lenses usually, but you may get fairly good ones.

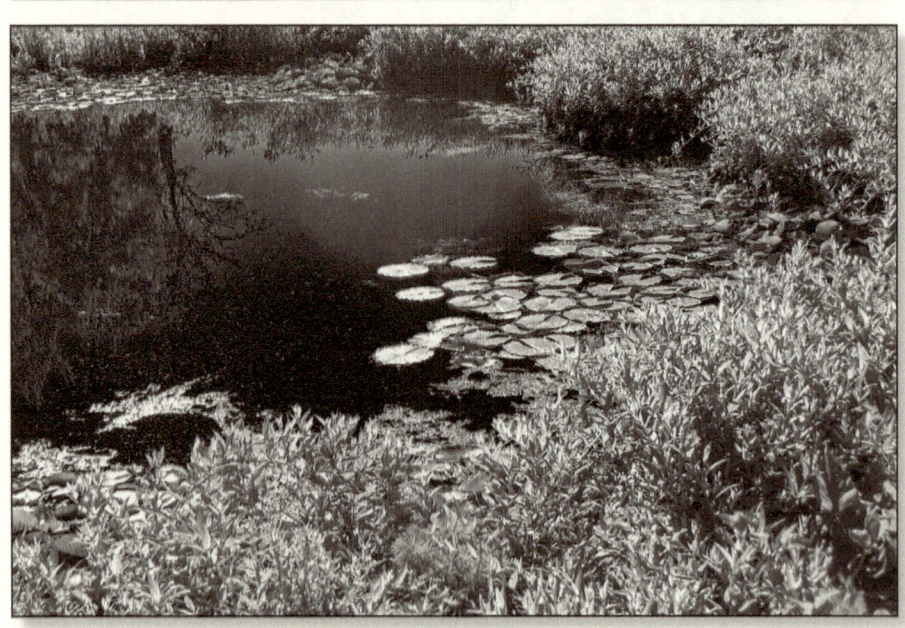

The lake, Ballston Lake, N.Y., July 11, 2014.
Canon EOS 20D, 28mm, 1/1250, f/4.5, ISO 200, Tv, pattern metering
Photo © 2014, 2015 by Shawn M. Tomlinson

For example, when I bought the Canon EOS 10D from KEH, I knew the lenses there would be a bit more expensive, so I started nosing around eBay and Goodwill websites.

I found an early Canon EOS Rebel autofocus film SLR and placed a bid. Including shipping — which is inordinately high on the Goodwill site — it cost $35 for the camera and lens. And the lens, a Canon EF II 28-80mm f/3.5-5.6, was in nearly perfect shape.

I used it all the time on the 20D (my 10D, sadly, died, so I replaced it with the 20D) until I purchased a Canon EF II 50mm f/1.8 lens. A zoom lens

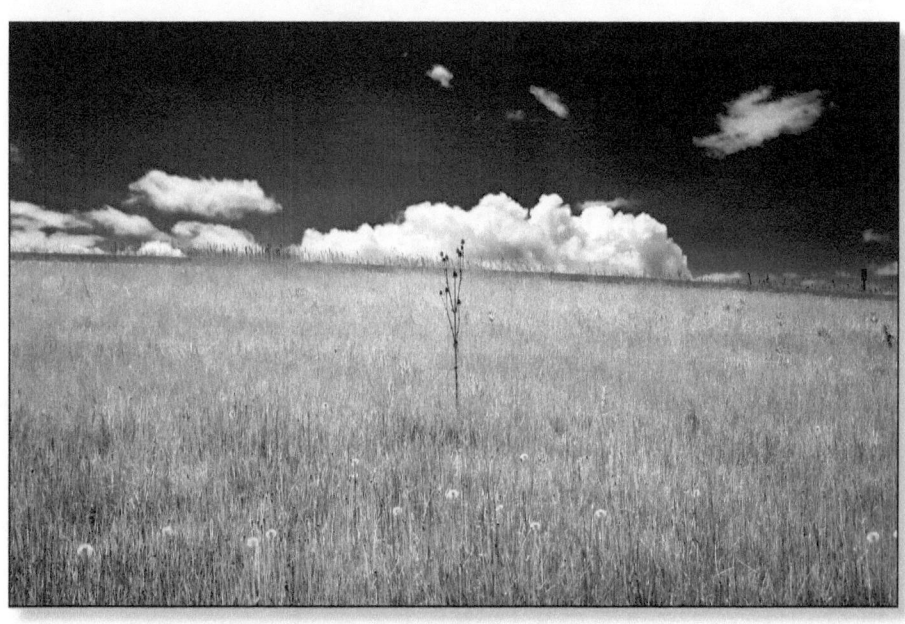

Rotterdam, N.Y., May 31, 2014.
Nikon D1x, 28mm, 1/4000, f/3.5, ISO 200, Av, pattern metering
Photo © 2014, 2015 by Shawn M. Tomlinson

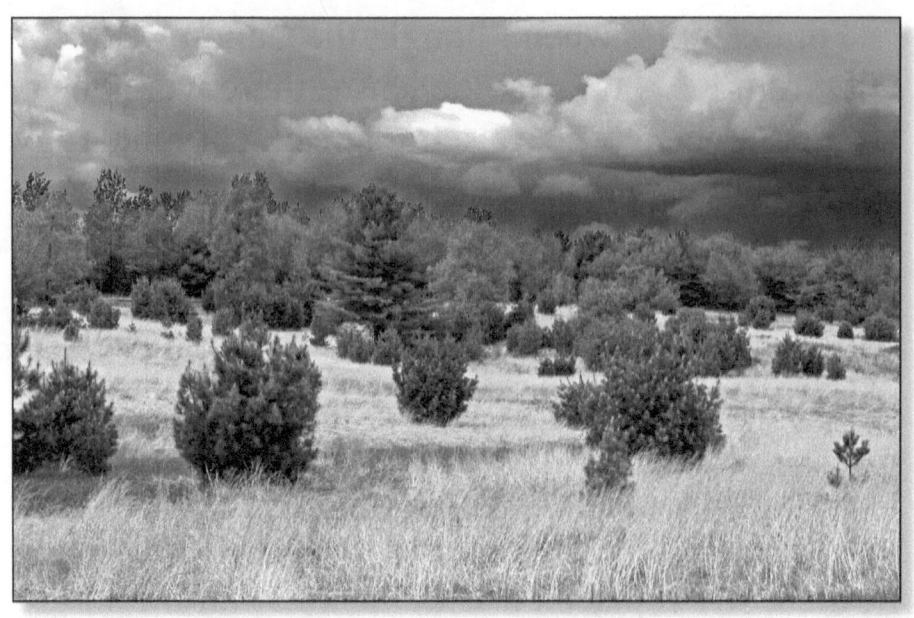

Broadalbin, N.Y., May 23, 2014.
Nikon D1, 44mm, 1/2500, f/5.6, ISO 400, Av, pattern metering
Photo © 2014, 2015 by Shawn M. Tomlinson

can't compare with a prime or fixed focal length lens and, hey, I am having a love affair with primes on all my cameras.

The 28-80mm lens, though, is sharp with little distortion or chromatic aberration, but it is a kit lens and thus, not the best. I needed to get the better prime lens for the 20D, but the 28-80mm still works fine.

You can even tough it out and get a manual — non-autofocus — lens for the Nikon or Pentax, but not the Canon. Manual lenses usually are cheaper than autofocus lenses. They take a little more time and skill — and patience — to use, but, especially if you find a 50mm f/1.8, you have a spectacular lens that will produce very sharp images. Lenses made by and for Nikon and Pentax from the early 1970s onward will work on all modern Nikon and Pentax DSLR cameras respectively. Canon, however, changed its lens mount when the company made the switch to autofocus, so manual FD lenses will not work on Canon DSLRs without an expensive adapter that rarely is worth the price. Canon

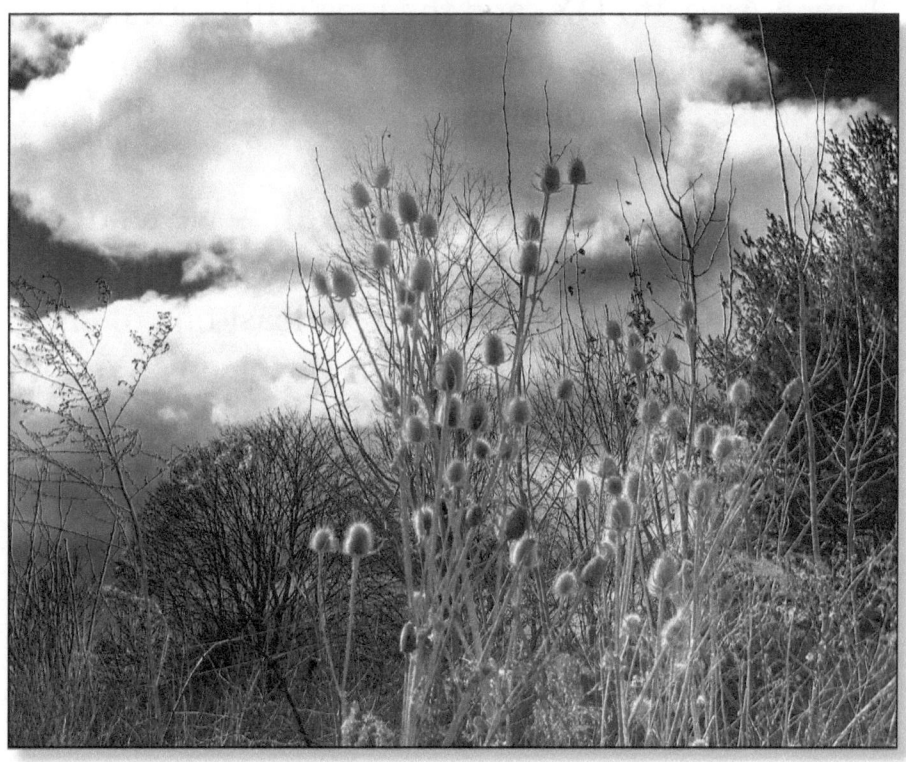

Saratoga Springs, N.Y., April 5, 2014.
Canon EOS 10D, 48mm, 1/250, f/11, ISO 200, P, pattern metering
Photo © 2014, 2015 by Shawn M. Tomlinson

changed its lens mount again for its "digital" lens line, so anything labeled EF-S will not fit or work on a Canon EOS D30, D60 or 10D. Only the EF lenses will. EF lenses actually will work on all Canon DSLRs, full frame or crop sensor.

Nikon has a bit of the same with its "DX" lenses. They are made to cover the smaller APS-C sensors found in the company's low to mid-range cameras, but not the full-frame sensors. So, if you put a "DX" lens on, say, a D4S, your images will have black corners, but the lens will mount. Switch the "Image Area" to DX, and the lens will work fine.

Canon makes its lens mounts dummy proof. EF-S lenses will not physically mount on full-frame cameras.

As photographers — at any level — we tend to like photographic equipment, so the only thing usually keeping us from having at least one of each DSLR body and one of each lens is the cost. Yet, it is important for any serious photographer — at any level — to have at least two camera bodies because these are sophisticated, complicated, modern electronic devices with far too many possible glitches and failures to predict.

You may not need 12 DSLR bodies like I have, but two is a good start.

— *SMT, July 4, 2015*

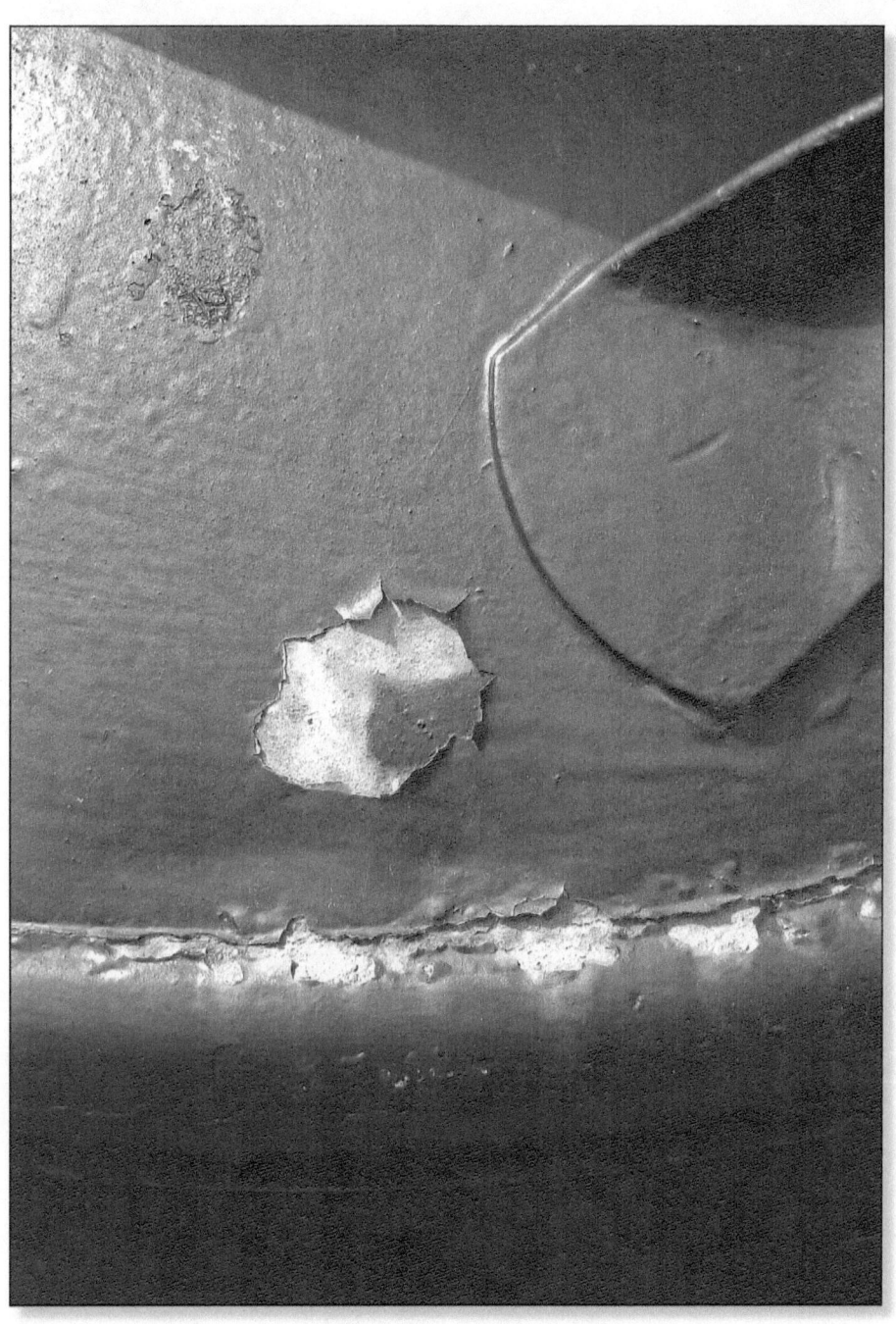

Ballston Lake, N.Y., April 11, 2014.
Nikon D1, 80mm, 1/1000, f/5.6, ISO 1600, Av, spot metering
Photo © 2014, 2015 by Shawn M. Tomlinson

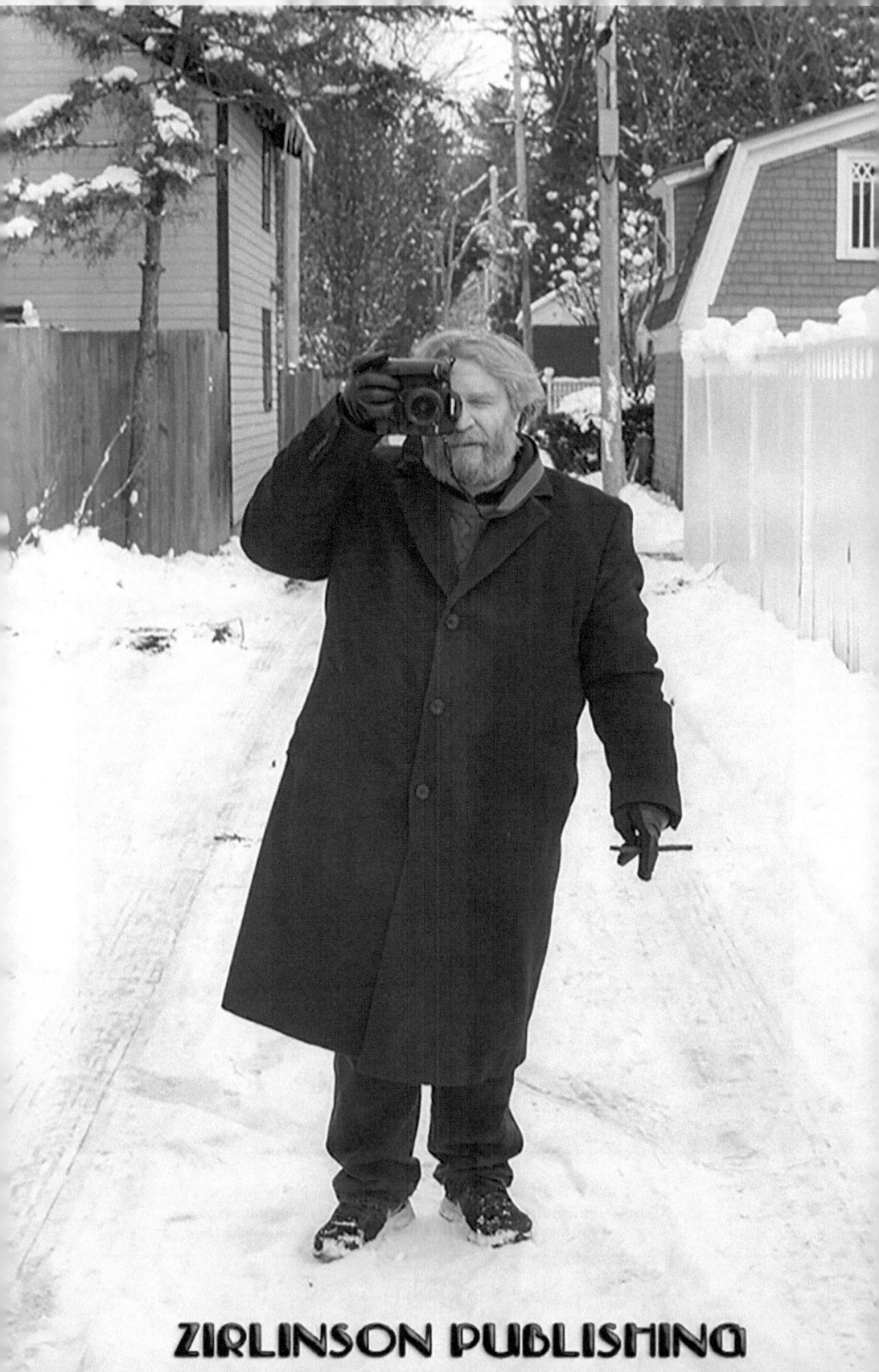

ZIRLINSON PUBLISHING

Photography

The Workhorse DSLR

Revisiting the Canon EOS 20D

hawn M. Tomlinson's

Photography:
The Old Workhorse DSLR

Revisiting the Canon EOS 20D

Shawn M. Tomlinson's
Guide to Photography
Volume 8

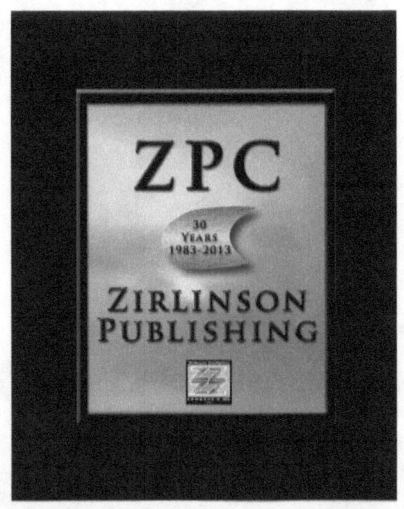

The Workhorse DSLR

Revisiting the Canon EOS 20D

Shawn M. Tomlinson's
Guide to Photography
Volume 8

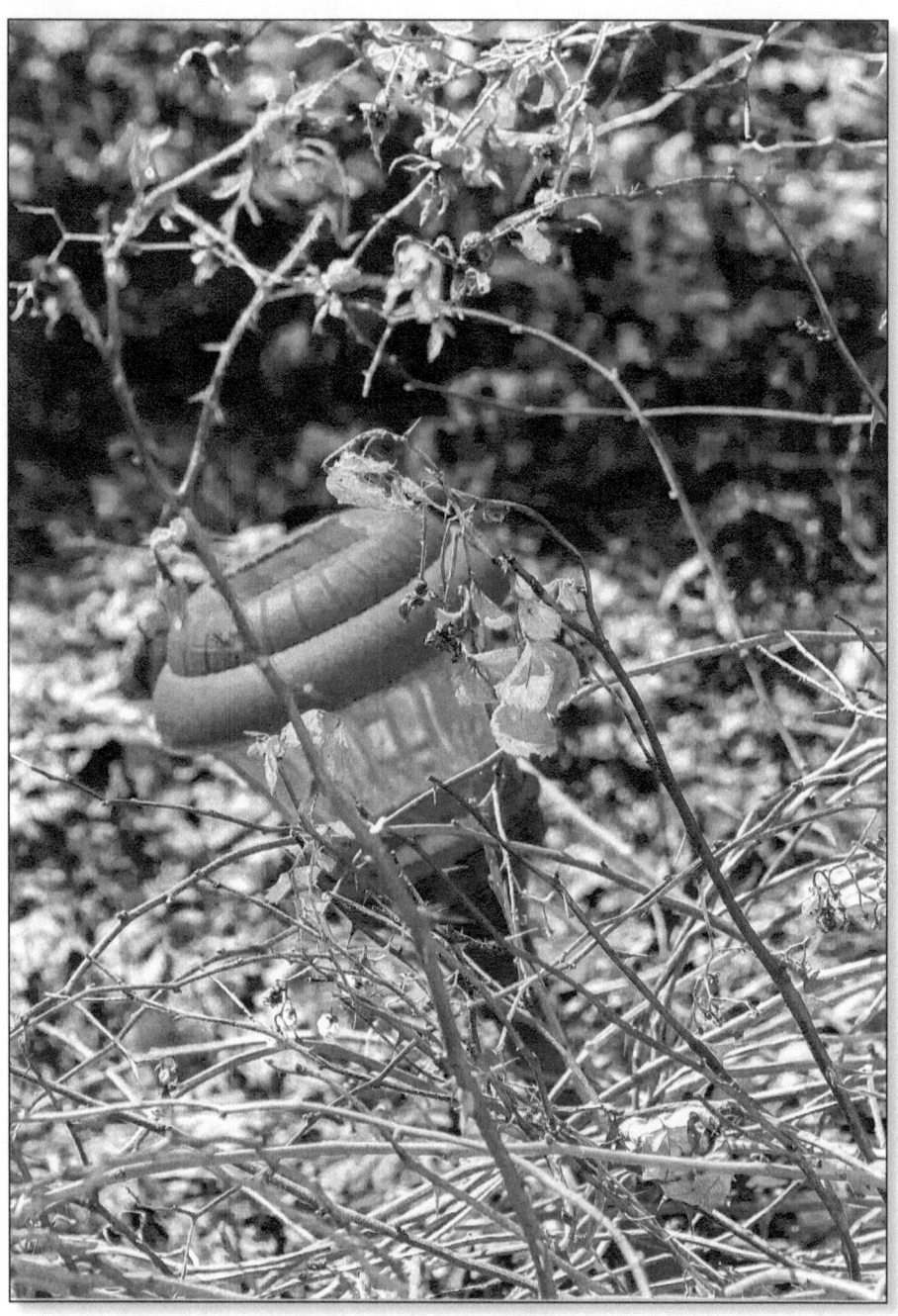

Ballston Lake, N.Y., April 21, 2014.
Canon EOS 20D, 200mm, 1/800, f/11, ISO 1600, P, pattern metering
Photo © 2014, 2015 by Shawn M. Tomlinson

First Words

I love old cameras.

This is true for film cameras, of course, but it's also true for digital single-lens reflex cameras as well.

The biggest difference between the two is that film cameras are just as good now as they were when they were brand new, assuming everything works properly. Put a good lens on a Nikon F from 1959 and load some good film — if you can find some — and the images you take will be just as good as during the heyday.

This is because the image capture media — film — improved right up until many companies stopped making it and it works wonders in SLRs.

DSLRs, however, use a fixed sensor, so the image quality remains the same for the life of the camera. Oh, you can put a really great lens on an old DSLR and it will shine, but it still does not have the resolution or technological advancements that continue to evolve year after year.

All that said, old DSLRs still have life left in them and many still produce fantastic images. I would, in fact, defy anyone to tell me the difference between an image shot with a DSLR made in 2004

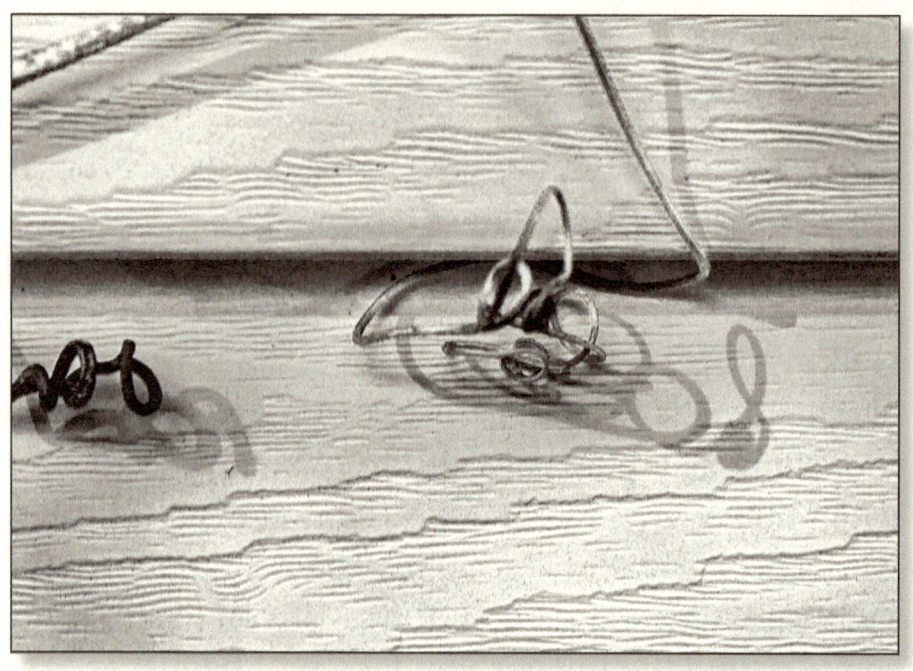

Ballston Lake, NY, May 6, 2014
Canon EOS 20D, 80mm, 1/200, f/8, ISO 200, P, pattern metering
© 2014, 2015 by Shawn M. Tomlinson

from one made in 2014 without using lab tests. Just looking at an image at a normal size on a computer display or on an 8.5-by-11-inch print, very few people can see the difference between 6 megapixels and 24 megapixels.

Marketing maneuvers have made people think they see a difference, but unless a photo shot at 6-megapixel resolution is enlarged beyond, say, 13-by-19 inches, most people can't.

I shoot images every day — with a variety of DSLRs; occasionally with a film SLR — and I would have a hard time making the distinction at a glance.

It is for this reason that I and other photographers like to shoot with older DSLRs. As long as they work properly, they're still great photographic tools.

Take for example, the Canon EOS 20D. It was a spectacular mid-range DSLR when it was introduced in 2004. It was so good in fact that Canon based its entire line of mid-range cameras on it for years to come. When the company changed too many things with the 60D, many people didn't like it and stuck with their older 30D, 40D or 50D, or some even with the 20D. The 70D went back to some of the basics of the pre-60D DSLRs, but with modern improvements. To get the build quality of the 20D, you need at least a Canon EOS 7D or 7D Mark II.

Still, it all comes back to the 20D.

It was and is a workhorse of a DSLR, mostly metal and rugged, and it produces spectacular images.

I use mine frequently.

Sure, it has a little more grain than my newer DSLRs, but grain is not a bad thing. The colors are fantastic, as are those produced by most Canon cameras.

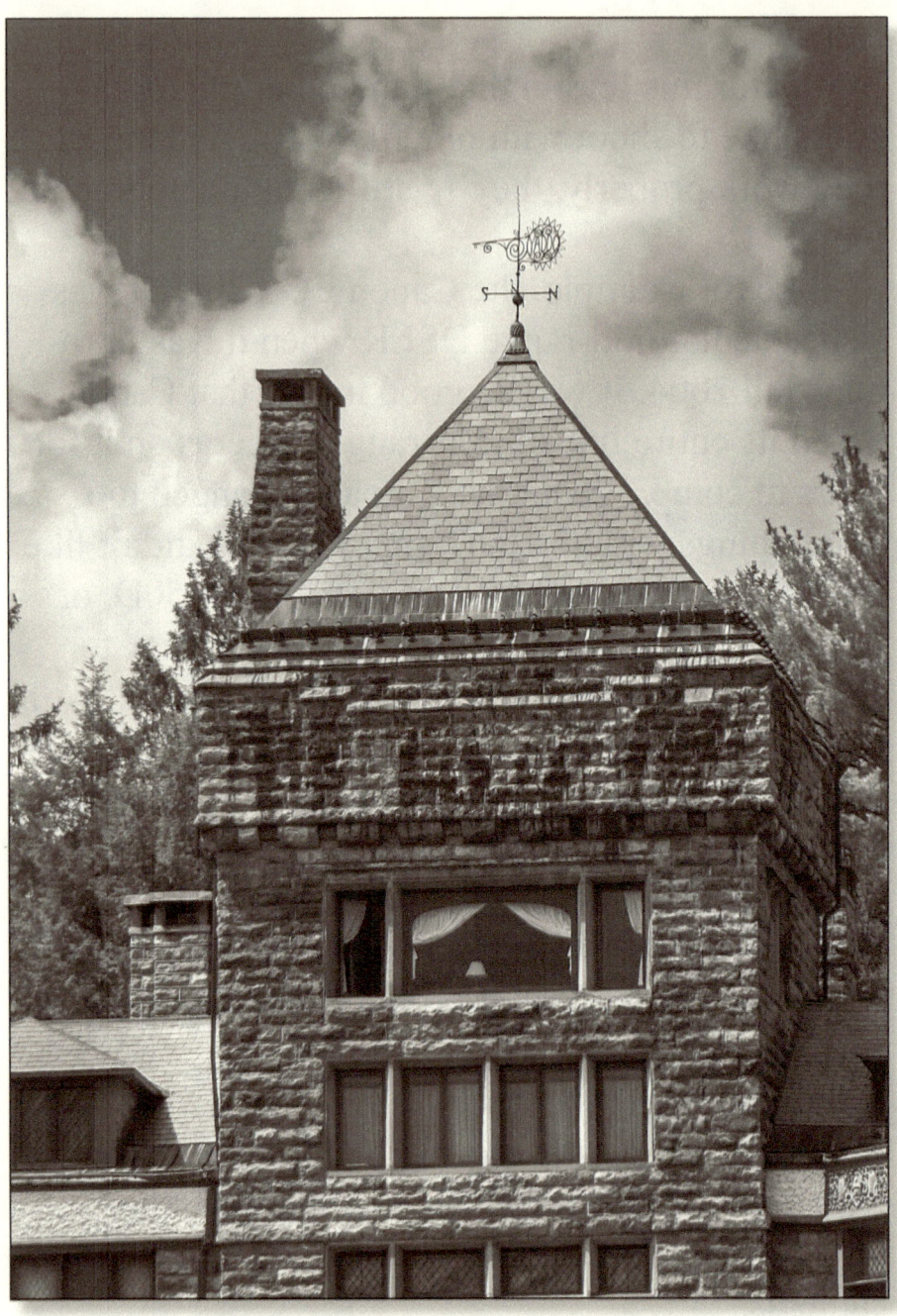

Yaddo, Saratoga Springs, NY, May 10, 2014
Pentax K20D, 200mm, 1/350, f/8, ISO 100, P, pattern metering
© 2014, 2015 by Shawn M. Tomlinson

Part 1
Why Would I Want an Old Camera?

The short answer is: They're good and they're cheap.

A little history first about Canon DSLR cameras.

Canon was the first camera manufacturer to release a consumer-level DSLR, the D30, in 2000. It had 3 megapixels and yet was a capable, great

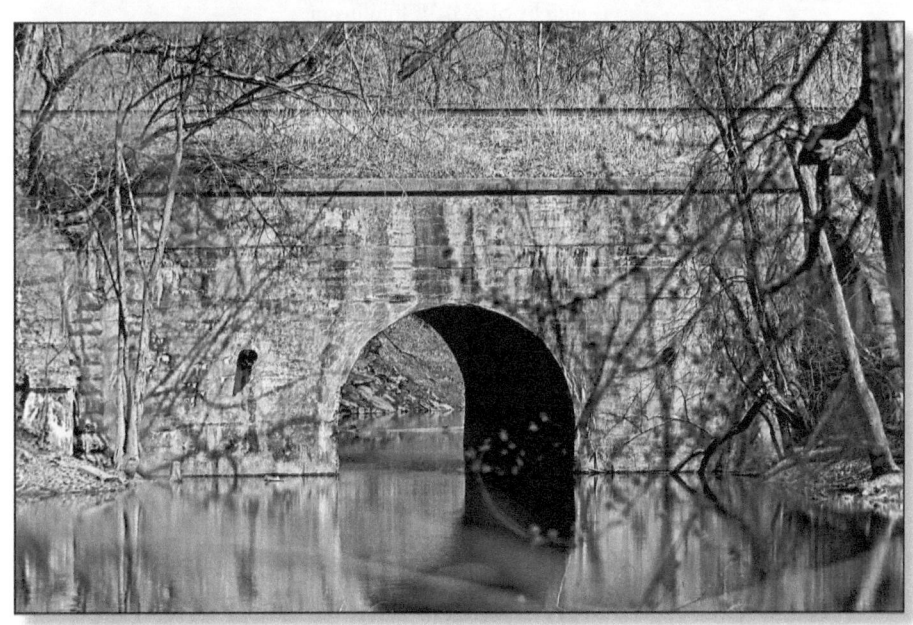

Quinlan Park, Scotia, N.Y., April 21, 2014.
Canon EOS 20D, 200mm, 1/250, f/6.3, ISO 100, P, pattern metering
Photo © 2014, 2015 by Shawn M. Tomlinson

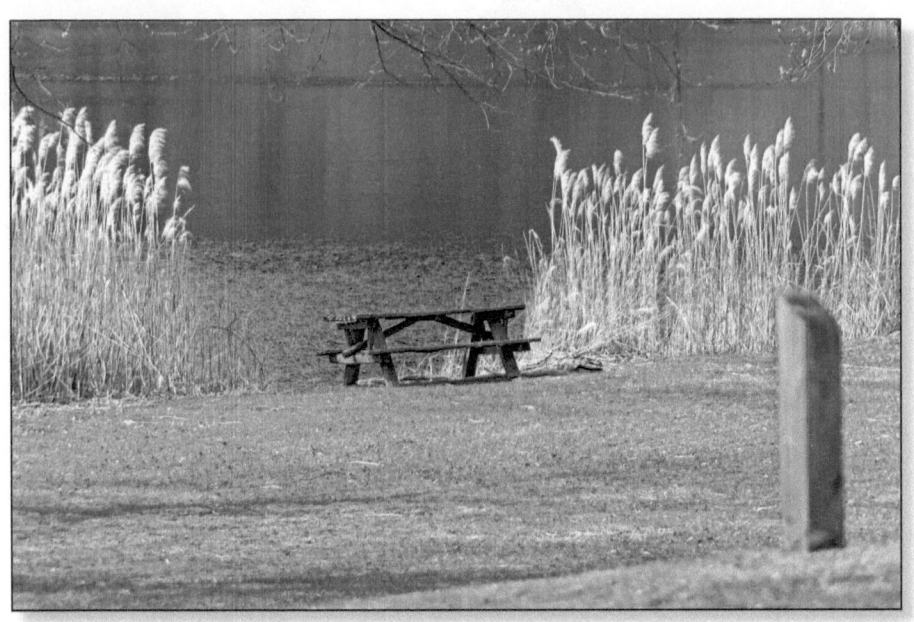

Quinlan Park, Scotia, N.Y., April 21, 2014.
Canon EOS 20D, 200 mm (320 mm), 1/200, f/5.6, ISO 100, P, pattern.
© 2015 by Shawn M. Tomlinson

camera allowing photographers who were not rich, full-time pros to move to digital. Two years later, Canon doubled the resolution with the D60, and a year later made many improvements to produce the Canon EOS 10D.

The 10D was my first Canon DSLR, purchased not long ago for $69 including a battery grip. A lot less than the 2003 price of $1,500. I really loved the 10D. I'd never seen such great color straight out of the camera.

I'd be using it still except that it died and I replaced it with the 20D. I also would recommend the

10D except for two things: 1) It will not accept Canon EF-S "digital" lenses, so it is difficult to get really wide-angle shots; and 2) it has a terribly long start-up time, from power on or from sleep. It gets annoying. Great photos, though.

So, the 20D is the oldest Canon DSLR in the mid-

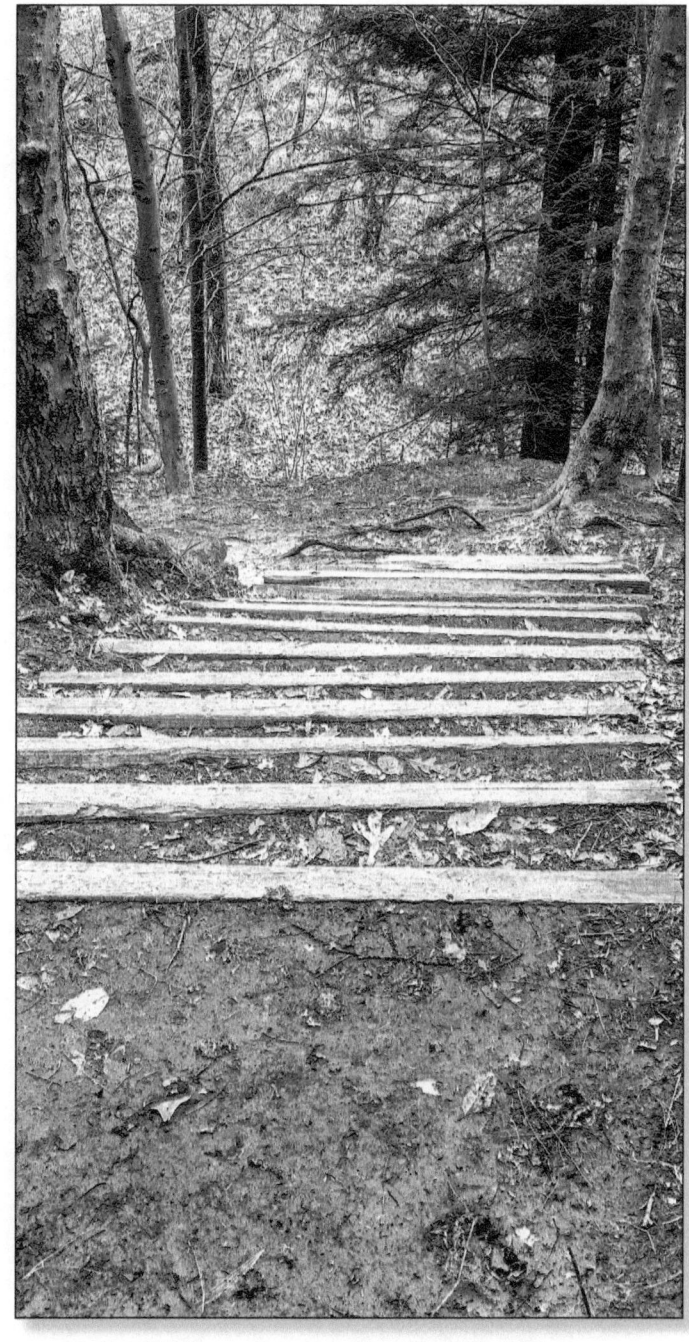

Indian Kill Nature Preserve, Glenville, N.Y., April 23, 2014.
Canon EOS 20D, 28 mm (44.2 mm), 1/50, f/16, ISO 400, A-DEP, pattern.
© 2015 by Shawn M. Tomlinson

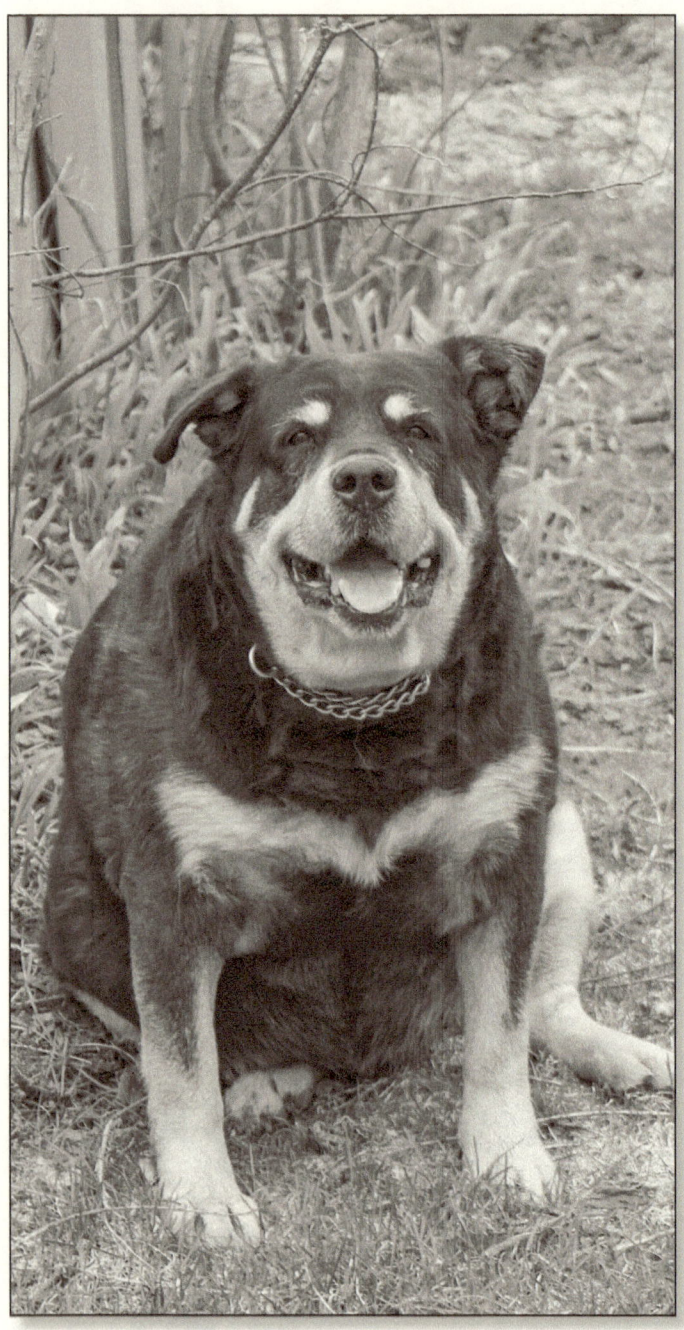

Baby, Ballston Lake, N.Y., April 25, 2014.
Canon EOS 20D, 80 mm (128 mm), 1/100, f/5.6, ISO 400, P, pattern.
© 2015 by Shawn M. Tomlinson

range category that is considered a "modern" DSLR. It powers on virtually instantly, and wakes from sleep immediately.

It has the solid build of the 10D, and it improves upon the 10D's 6.1-megapixel resolution slightly to 8.2 megapixels.

The reasons to buy and

use a Canon EOS 20D remain the same as stated at the top of this section. It is solid, works well under most conditions, provides great photos and generally costs less than $100 for the camera body. A workmanlike lens can be had for less than $100 as well.

Considering the cost of a new mid-range DSLR — usually about $1,000 — you can't go wrong buying a 20D.

Even the entry-level, mostly plastic new DSLRs cost at least four times as much as a used 20D.

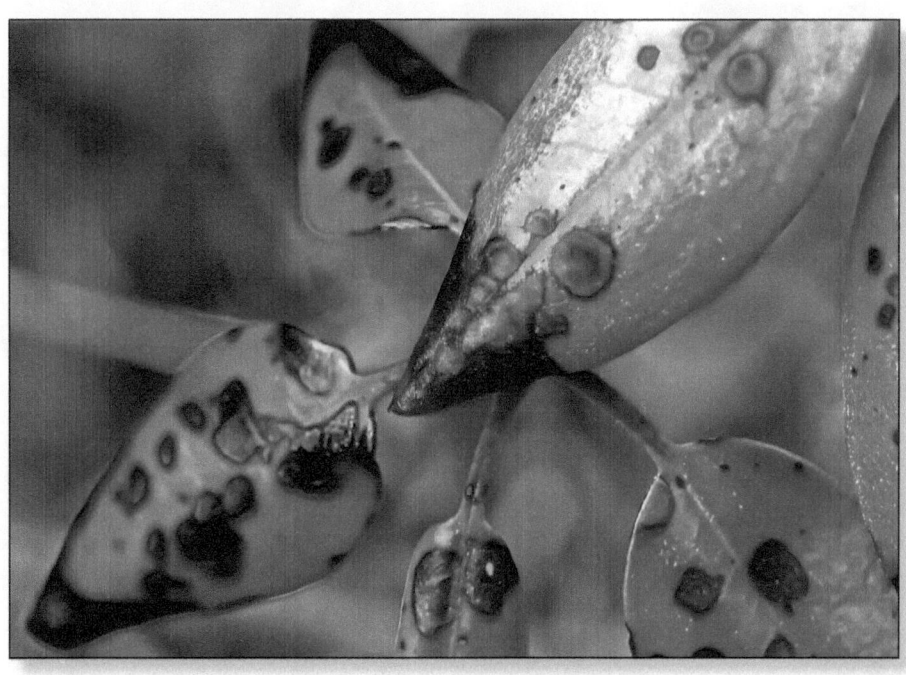

Ballston Lake, NY, May 6, 2014
Canon EOS 20D, 80mm, 1/80, f/5.6, ISO 200, P, pattern metering
© 2014, 2015 by Shawn M. Tomlinson

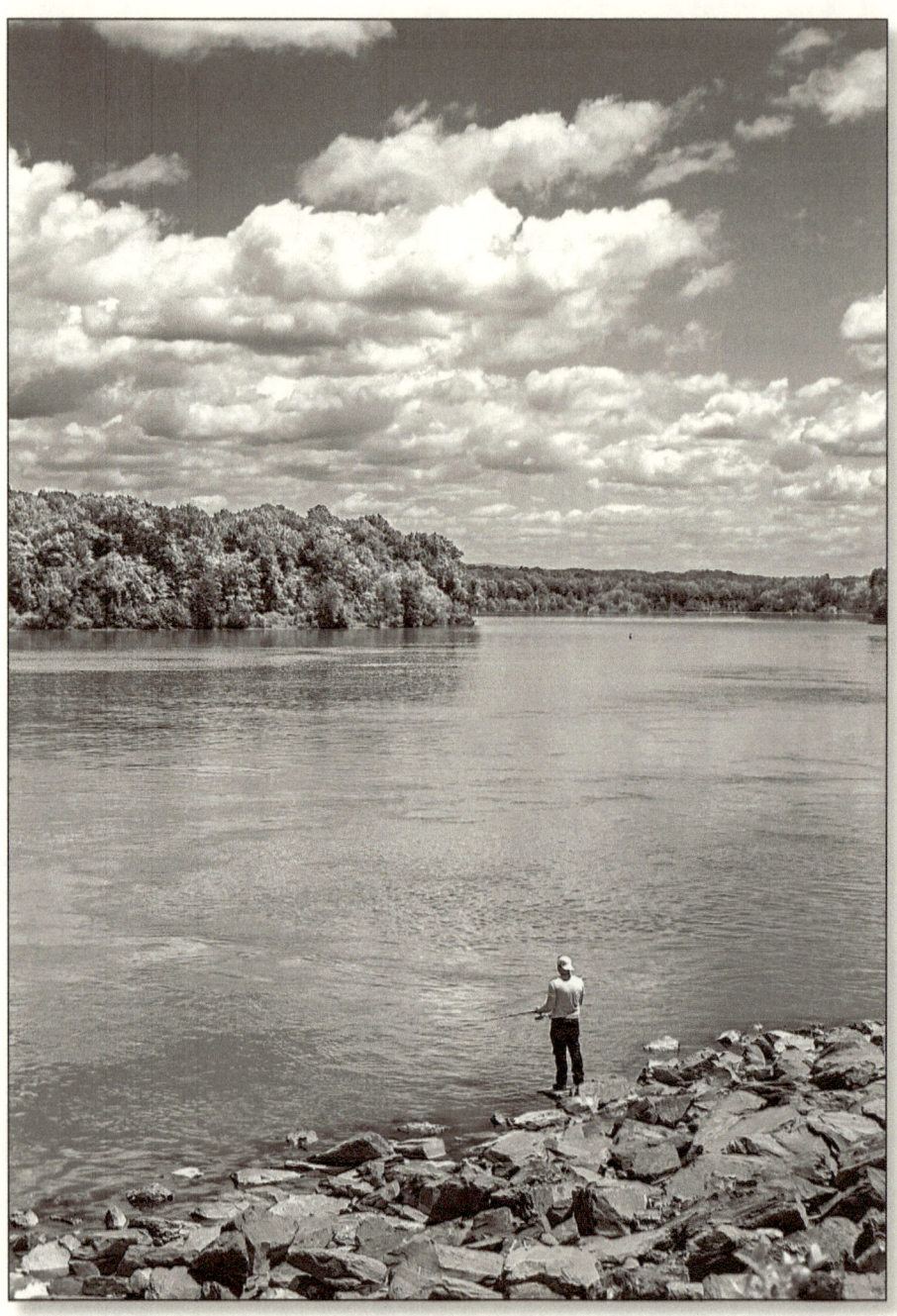

Cohoes, NY, June 7, 2014
Canon EOS 20D, 28mm, 1/2000, f/3.5, ISO 200, S, pattern metering
© 2014, 2015 by Shawn M. Tomlinson

Part 2
Canon EOS 20D
Capabilities

The basics first for the Canon EOS 20D:

- Resolution — 8.2 megapixels (more than enough for most photographers)
- Mount — EF and EF-S
- Frames per second — 5 fps
- ISO range — 100 to 3200
- Shutter speeds — 30 seconds to 1/8000th of a second
- Focus points — 9
- Body material — magnesium alloy

Three of those statistics are particularly impressive for a 2004 DSLR made for enthusiast photographers rather than pros.

Five frames per second is remarkably fast. The most recent DSLR in the mid-range line from Canon only beats it by two. An current entry-level DSLR usually shoots at two to three fps.

What does this mean? It means you can hold the shutter button down and take five images in one second. Not that you would do it all the time, but the capability is impressive. And you will use it occasionally, just because you can.

The shutter speed range also is unusual, and much faster than entry-level DSLRs. 1/8000th of a second can freeze water in a fountain, make a bumble bee's wings sharp as glass and catch virtually any other motion you care to stop. Only pro cameras typically exceed this speed, and pros rarely use 1/16000th of a second anyway. Most entry-level DSLRs stop at 1/4000th of a second, which is fantastic, but not this good.

The other very impressive statistic is that mag-

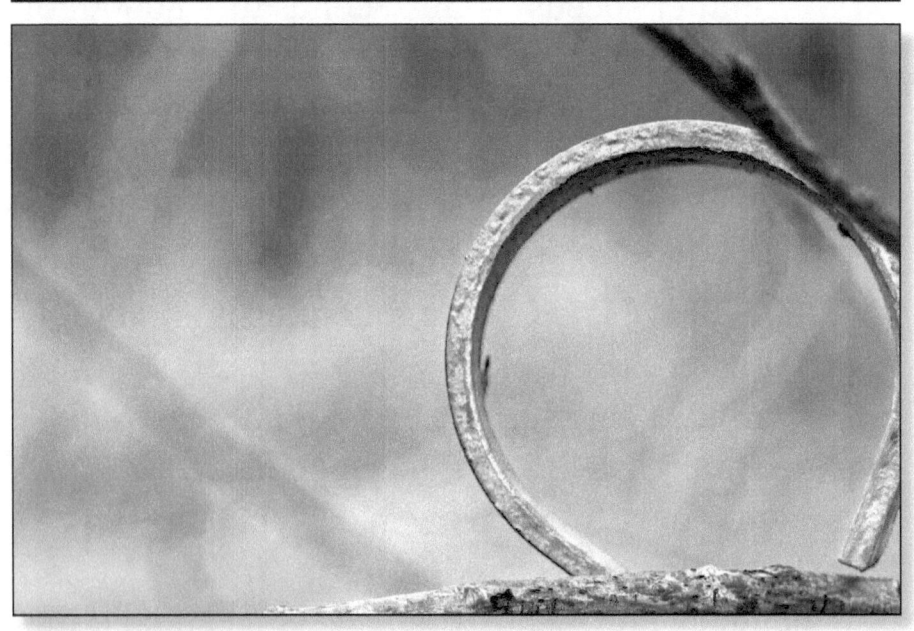

Ballston Lake, N.Y., April 25, 2014.
Canon EOS 20D, 80 mm (128 mm), 1/160, f/7.1, ISO 400, P, pattern.
© 2015 by Shawn M. Tomlinson

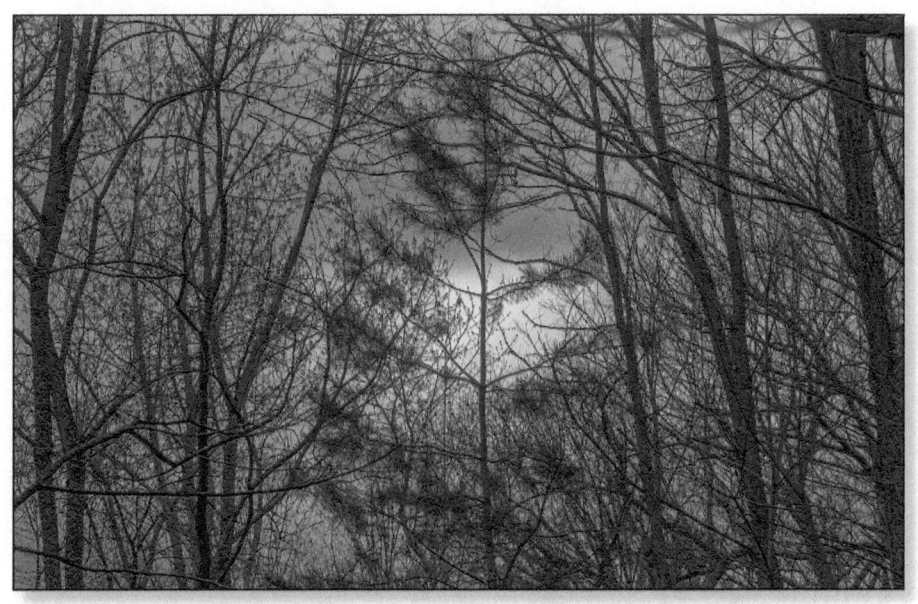

Indian Kill Nature Preserve, Glenville, N.Y., April 27, 2014.
Canon EOS 20D, 80 mm (128 mm), 1/400, f/11, ISO 200, P, pattern.
© 2015 by Shawn M. Tomlinson

nesium alloy build. No entry level DSLRs are built this tough, no matter how much they cost. To keep prices down, manufacturers substitute plastic. Tough, hard plastic, but plastic nonetheless. Metal means the 20D can take a beating.

To me, the Canon EOS 20D is a much better camera than, say a Canon EOS Rebel T3, and as a bonus, you don't have to have those embarrassing moments when people see the word "Rebel" on your mass-produced anything-but-rebellious DSLR camera.

All the technical stuff doesn't really matter much until you are shooting and need to do something unusual.

I rarely use 1/8000th of a second shutter speed, but then I was in an unusual garden with odd but bright light with this fantastic fountain in the middle. I decided this was the time to try it since I'd had mixed luck getting the water-freezing effect I wanted previously.

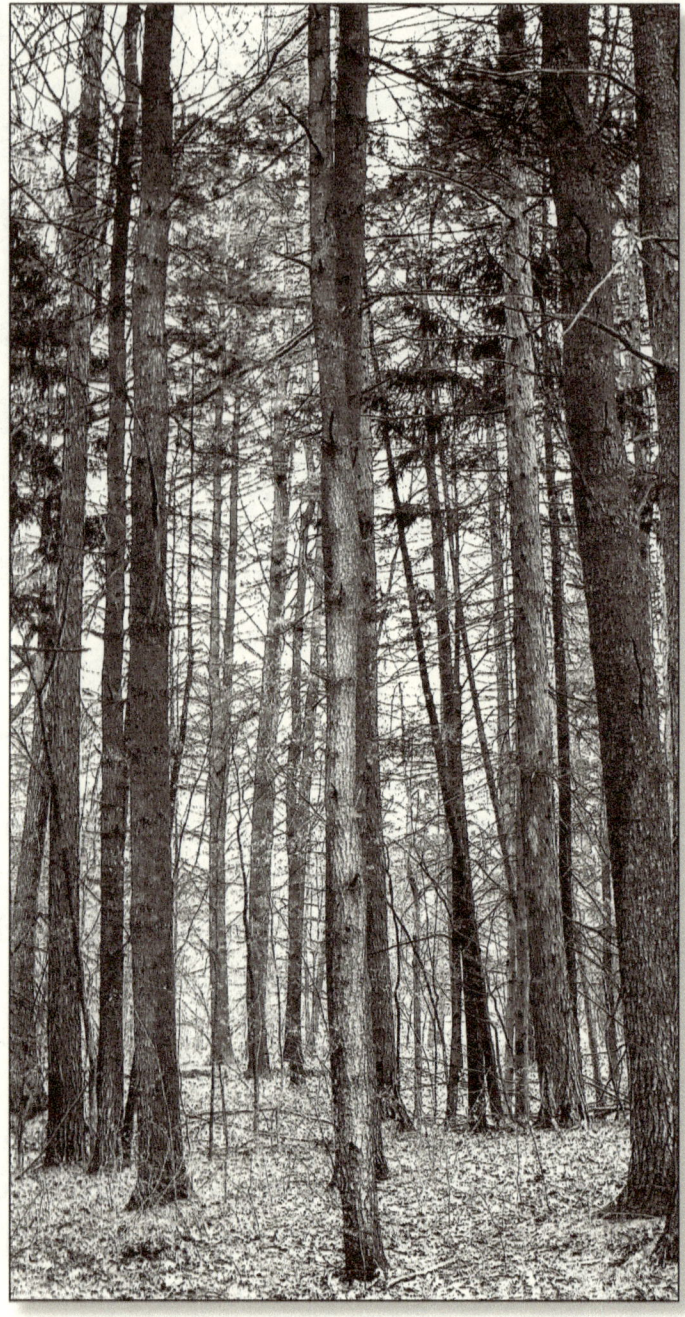

Yaddo, Saratoga Springs, N.Y., May 3, 2014.
Canon EOS 20D, 30 mm (48 mm), 1/125, f/7.1, ISO 200, P, pattern.
© 2015 by Shawn M. Tomlinson

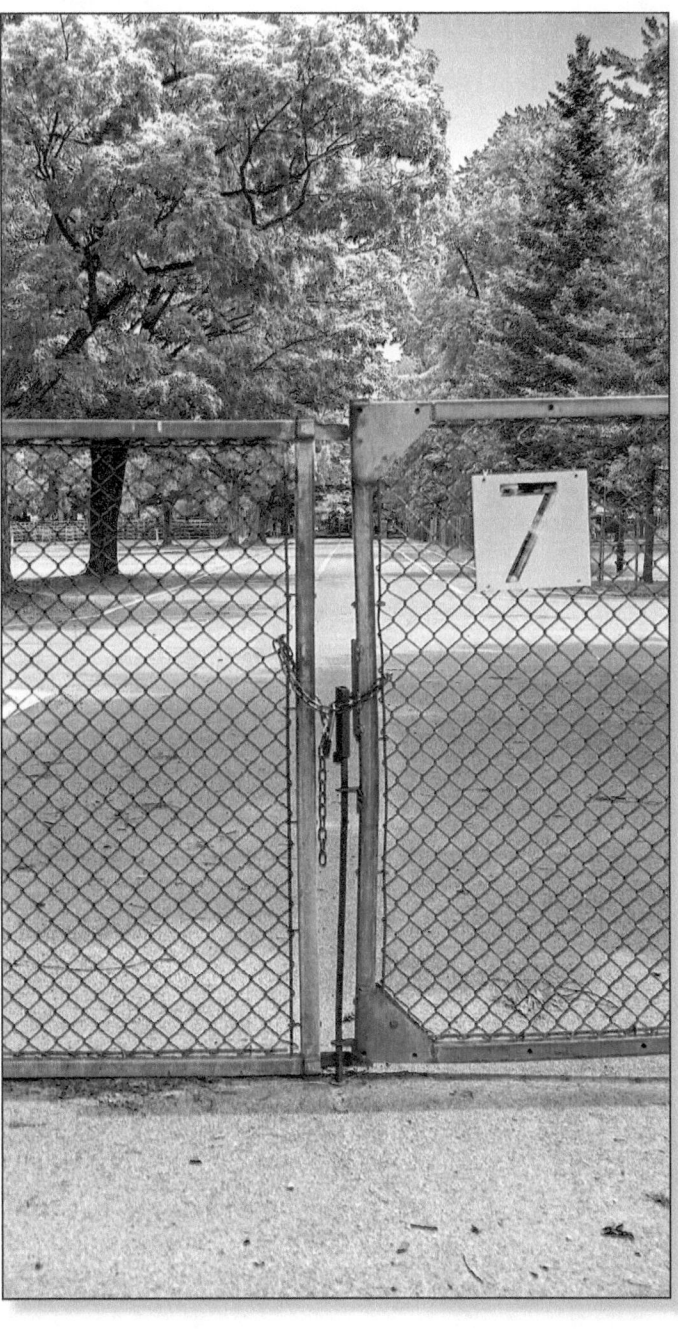

Oh, sure, I could freeze water droplets, but it never looked exactly like I intended it to. Sure enough, 1/8000th did the trick.

The truth is, though, that whether you're shooting in Program, Shutter-Priority, Aperture-Priority or Manual Mode, you will tend to

Saratoga Springs, NY, June 3, 2014
Canon EOS 20D, 28mm, 1/640, f/4, ISO 200, S, pattern metering
© 2014, 2015 by Shawn M. Tomlinson

use the same types of settings most of the time. It's great to know, though, that a $100 camera can do so much more.

Of course, this all is assuming you shoot **ONLY** in **RAW**. Shooting in JPEG defeats the purpose of using a DSLR camera. JPEG is a compressed file format that throws out bits of digital information to compress the files. The results include flat color, red-green-blue color noise, artifacts and a lot

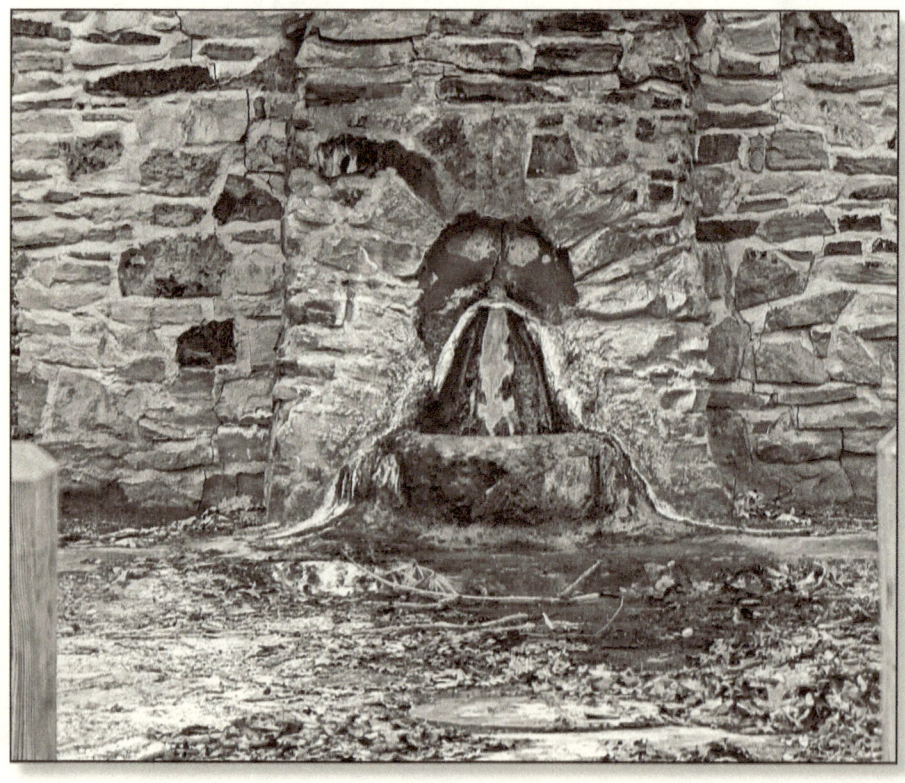

Saratoga Performing Arts Center, Saratoga Springs, N.Y., May 3, 2014.
Canon EOS 20D, 80 mm (128 mm), 1/100, f/6.3, ISO 200, P, pattern.
© 2015 by Shawn M. Tomlinson

of painful hair-pulling later when you realize you would have had the best photo ever taken in the history of photography... if only you had shot it in RAW.

RAW takes up more memory card space and hard drive space, but shooting in RAW means the camera records and keeps every last bit of data

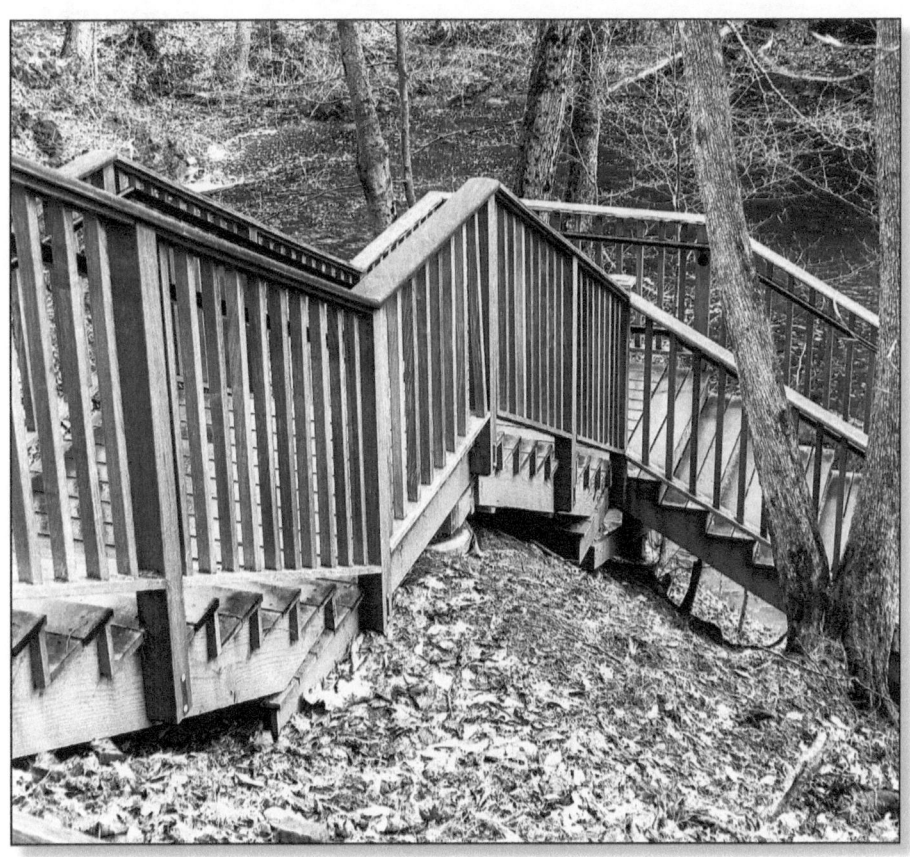

Saratoga Performing Arts Center, Saratoga Springs, N.Y., May 3, 2014.
Canon EOS 20D, 28 mm (44.2 mm), 1/125, f/5.6, ISO 400, A-DEP, pattern.
© 2015 by Shawn M. Tomlinson

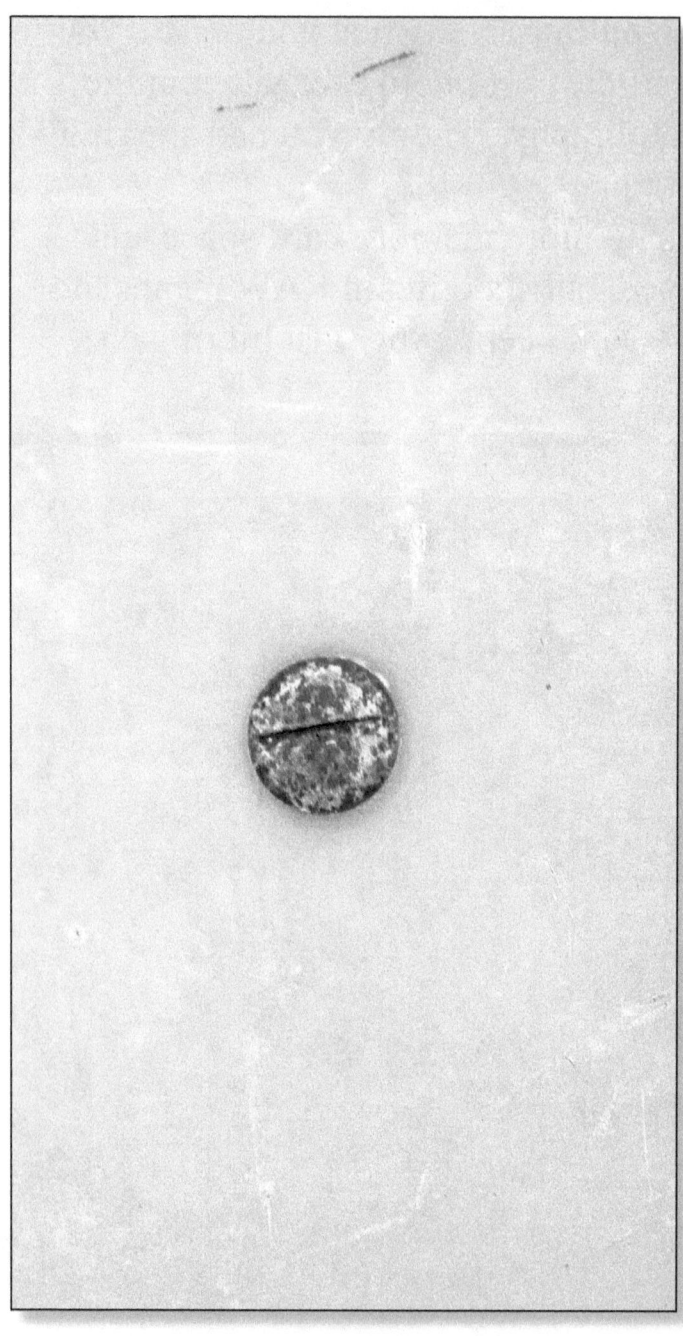

Ballston Lake, N.Y., April 25, 2014.
Canon EOS 20D, 80 mm (128 mm), 1/160, f/7.1, ISO 400, P, pattern.
© 2015 by Shawn M. Tomlinson

possible for that expo-sure. That means each file has far more possi-bilities for correction — color, exposure, shadows, highlights, saturation, clarity, etc. — than any JPEG.

Besides, your a ***photog-rapher***. If you could, you'd break off the JPEG switch so you could never touch it even by accident. The other rule I'm always on about is shooting at the **<u>lowest possible ISO sensitivity</u>** for your situation. Bright sun? ISO 200. Overcast? ISO 400. RARELY go higher than 400, especially on an older DSLR. Remember that grain I mentioned earlier? It gets much worse —

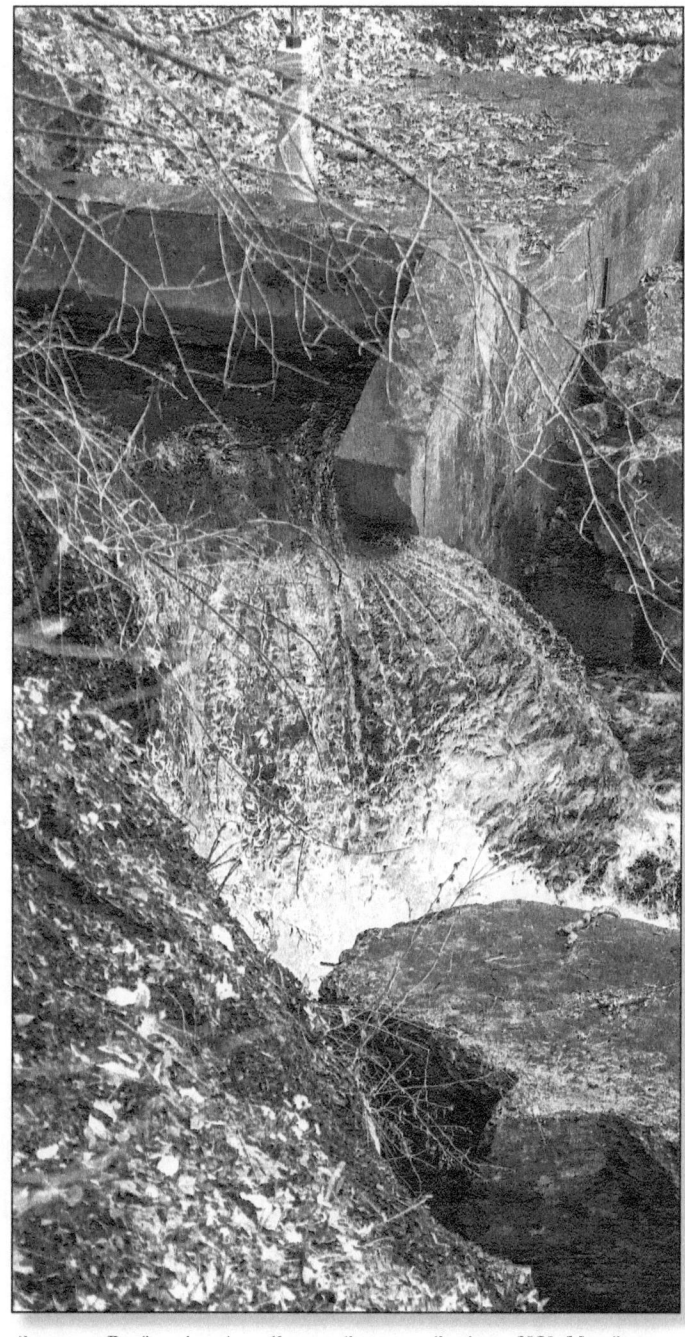

Saratoga Performing Arts Center, Saratoga Springs, N.Y., May 3, 2014.
Canon EOS 20D, 80 mm (128 mm), 1/1000, f/5.6, ISO 400, M, pattern.
© 2015 by Shawn M. Tomlinson

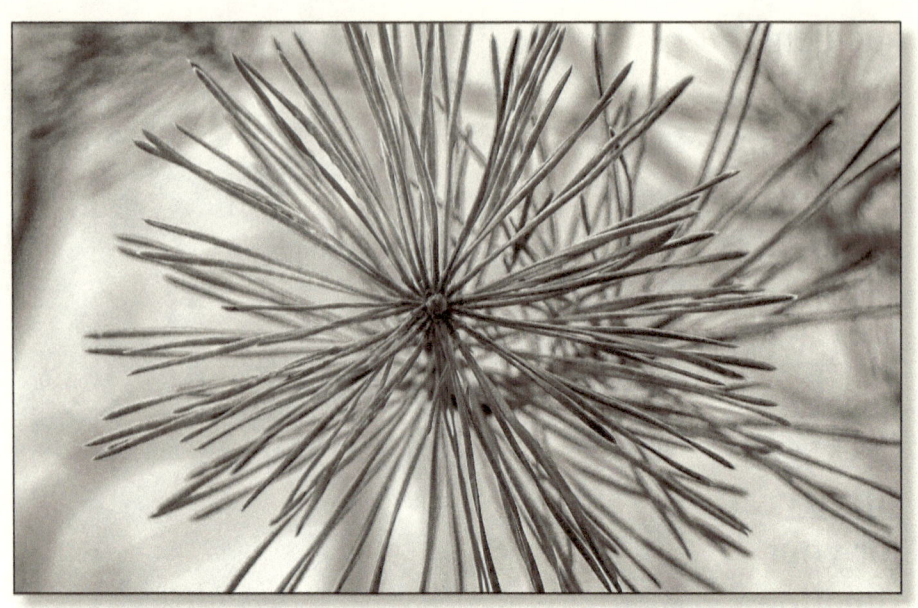

Indian Kill Nature Preserve, Glenville, N.Y., April 27, 2014.
Canon EOS 20D, 80 mm (128 mm), 1/250, f/9, ISO 200, P, pattern.
© 2015 by Shawn M. Tomlinson

as does the RGB noise — as the ISO numbers get higher. And the downside of ISO 100 is that you may lose a little of the dynamic range, meaning colors may appear a little flatter. (It does reduce grain, though.) Keeping that setting at ISO 200 most of the time is ideal.

Unless, of course, you live in Seattle or London or in the Northeastern United States in the winter when it's gray all the time. Then, well, ISO 400 is good. It gets you faster shutter speeds in crappy light and it doesn't add that much grain.

One other great capability of the Canon EOS

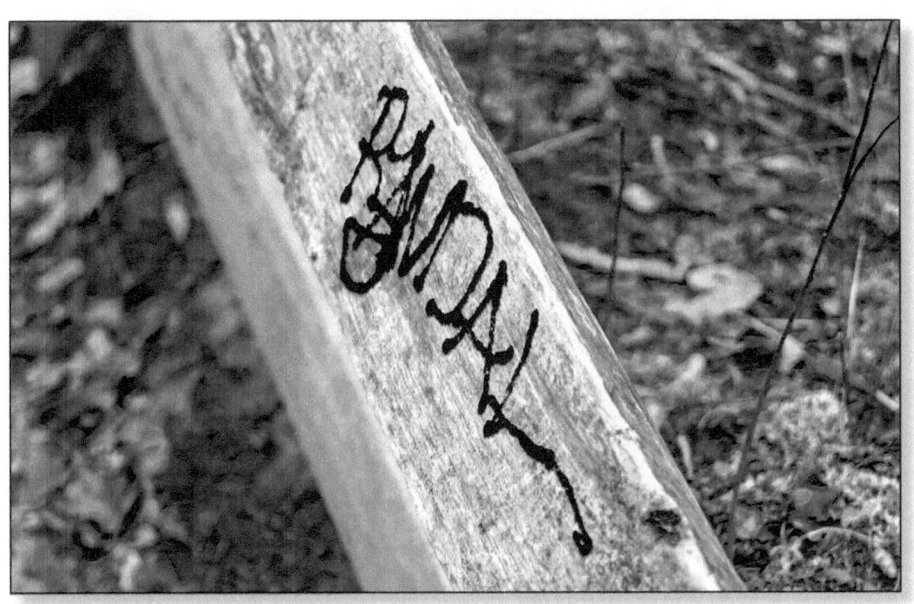

Indian Kill Nature Preserve, Glenville, N.Y., April 27, 2014.
Canon EOS 20D, 80 mm (128 mm), 1/125, f/6.3, ISO 200, P, pattern.
© 2015 by Shawn M. Tomlinson

20D and one that pros typically scoff at but is very useful is the A-DEP Mode setting. Since I wrote about this recently and put it fairly well, I'm quoting from my book, *Your 2nd DSLR: How & Why to Buy a 2nd Camera Body*: "A-DEP is a dummy feature for photographers too lazy to calculate effective depth-of-field. See, utilizing depth-of-field puts more subjects at different distances in focus in the same shot.

"When lenses still had aperture rings, we calculated DOF by focusing upon the farthest thing we wanted in focus and noting the distance number on the lens. Then we focused upon the nearest subject and noted that distance. Lenses also used to have DOF scales on them, so we looked at this while turning the focusing ring to the middle of the two focus values we noted earlier. These two distances lined up with numbers on the DOF scale. This told us the f-stop we needed to get the correct depth-of-field to get the nearest and farthest subjects in focus.

That's a bit complicated, but it works.

Without the DOF scale and without aperture rings, it's virtually impossible to do this with any accurate calculation.

So older Canons have the A-DEP Mode on the Mode dial. Set it, compose your scene and the camera uses its multiple focus points to do all that calculating stuff. Canon cameras still have this Mode, but it's harder to get to, which makes the Canon EOS 20D and a few others better for me when I want to use A-DEP. The elimination of easy access to this Mode makes newer models a little less of use to me."

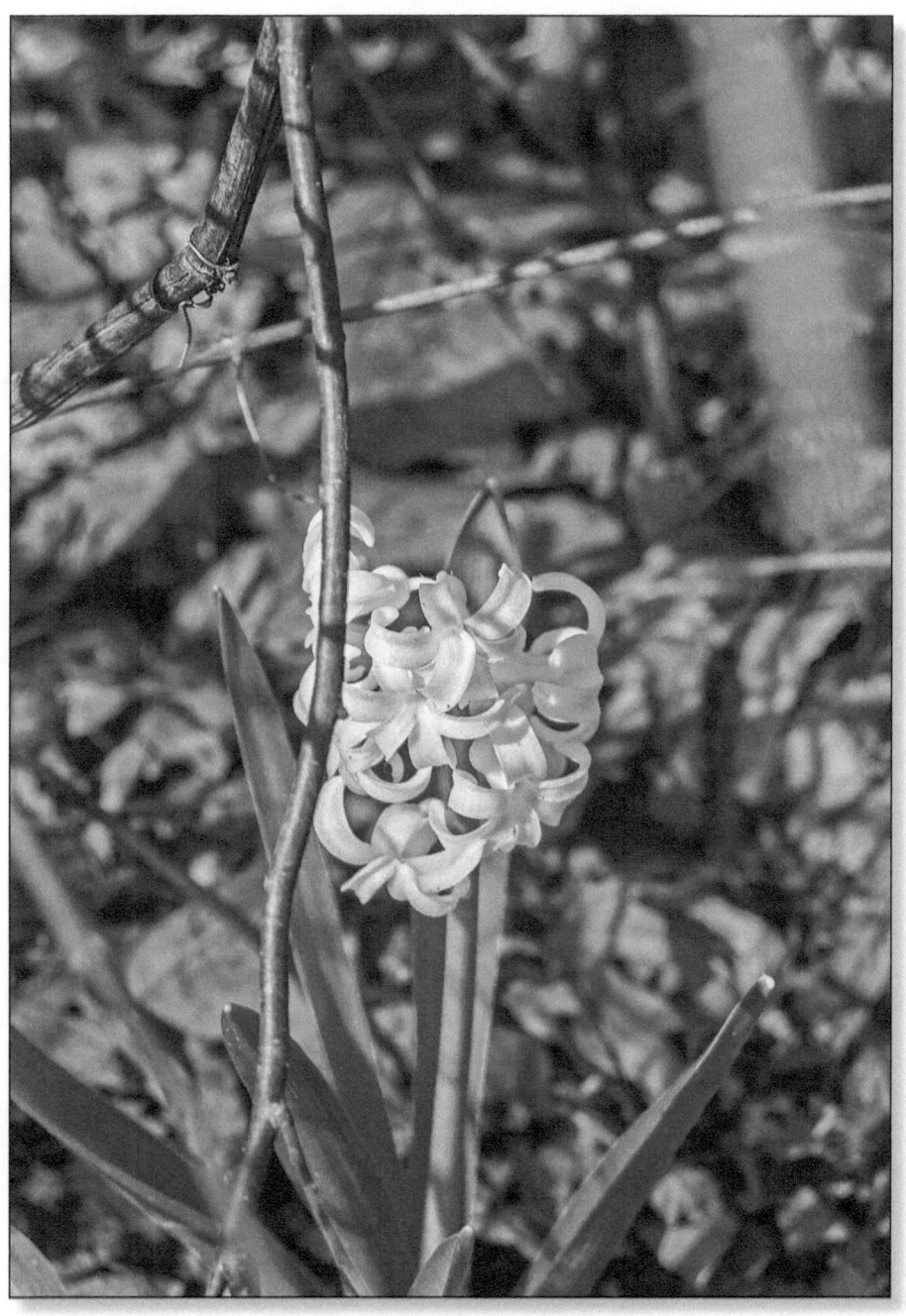

Ballston Lake, NY, May 1, 2014
Canon EOS 20D, 80mm, 1/250, f/9, ISO 200, P, pattern metering
© 2014, 2015 by Shawn M. Tomlinson

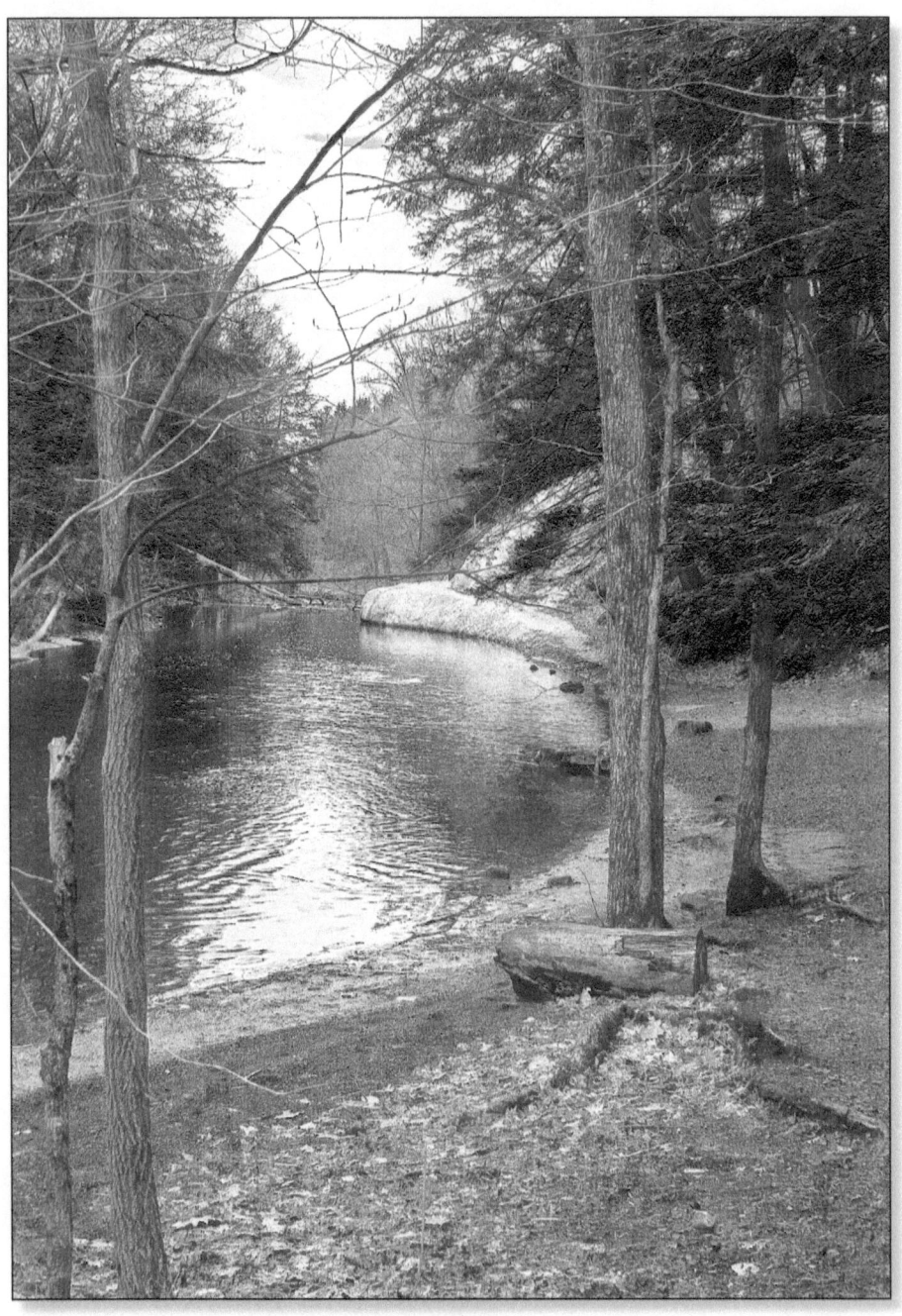

Saratoga Performing Arts Center, Saratoga Springs, N.Y., May 3, 2014.
Canon EOS 20D, 28 mm (44.2 mm), 1/250, f/9, ISO 400, P, pattern.
© 2015 by Shawn M. Tomlinson

Part 3
Getting Started

So, picture this: You just got the Canon EOS 20D in the mail. It may be your first DSLR or it may be a second camera you just want to explore the world with.

You splurged, so you got the camera, a 50mm f/1.8 lens with a UV filter, two batteries, the charger and the battery grip, as well as a couple of 8gb CompactFlash (CF) memory cards (important because your local big box conglomerate store doesn't sell CF cards anymore).

Of course you got the blue-white-red Canon strap, too. Why not?

Canon has this great thing with its battery grips that, sadly, Nikon and Pentax do not. It has a probe thingy that sticks up inside the camera to connect where the battery normally would go. This does two things. It adds a little more stability to the DSLR-grip combination, and it more importantly puts both batteries inside the grip. This means you can pop both of them out easily to charge them without having to remove the grip from the camera. Not only is this more convenient, but the convenience itself means it's more likely you will charge both batteries.

OK, so, you charge up the batteries and while you wait, you put the UV filter on that stellar yet cheap 50mm lens because,

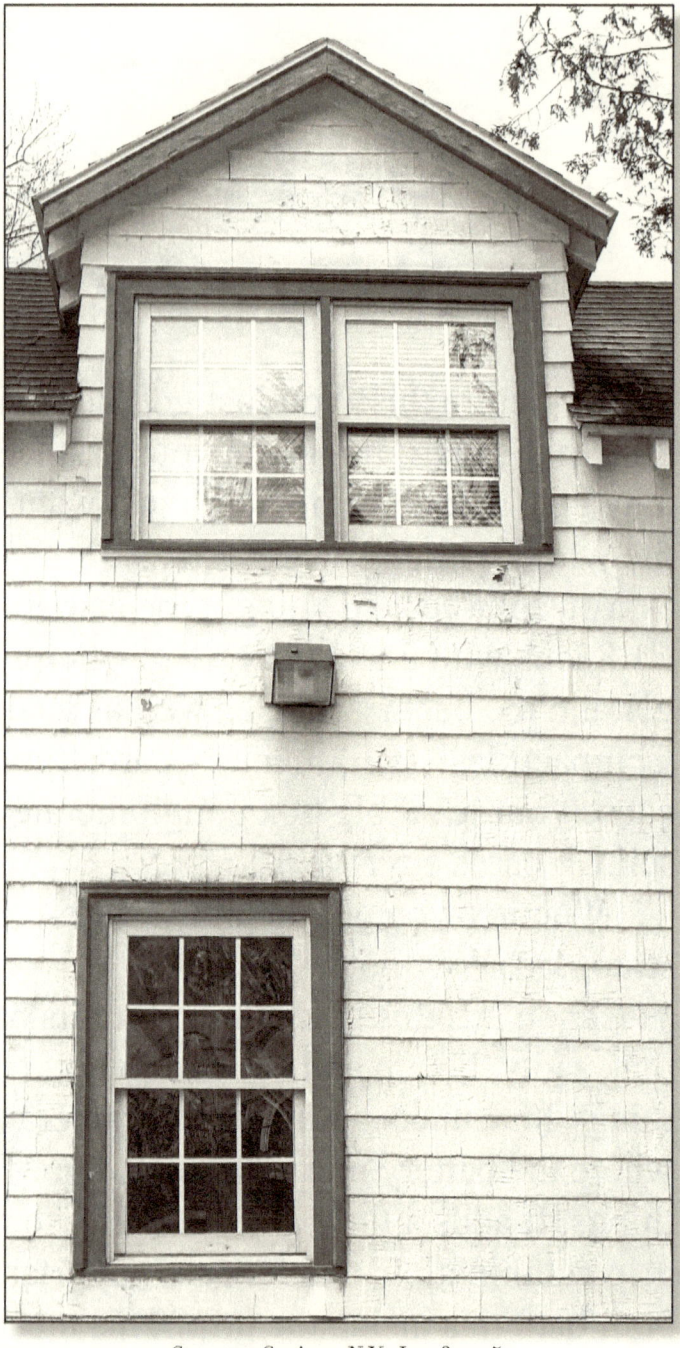

Saratoga Springs, N.Y., Jan. 3, 2015.
Canon EOS 20D, 28 mm (44.2 mm), 1/320, f/6.3, ISO 400, Tv, pattern.
© 2015 by Shawn M. Tomlinson

well, you should never use a lens without the filter. The UV filter's original use — to cut down ultraviolet light — isn't nearly as important as its newer function: protecting the front lens element. It's a lot cheaper to replace a UV filter than a lens.

And, of course, being a photographer rather than a snapshot shooter, you never use a lens cap. Lens caps are for amateurs and they only protect the lens when you're not using it. Lens caps, if you try to use them between every shot, will cut down your speed and you will lose some great shots while you're fumbling to get the cap off. Not for long, of course, because most people lose lens caps relative-

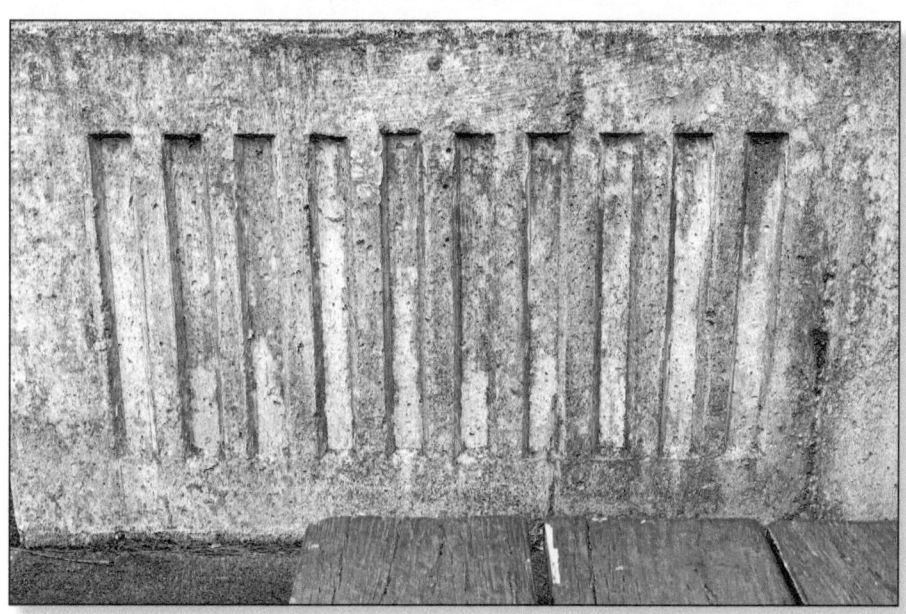

Saratoga Performing Arts Center, Saratoga Springs, N.Y., May 3, 2014.
Canon EOS 20D, 28 mm (44.2 mm), 1/250, f/10, ISO 400, P, pattern.
© 2015 by Shawn M. Tomlinson

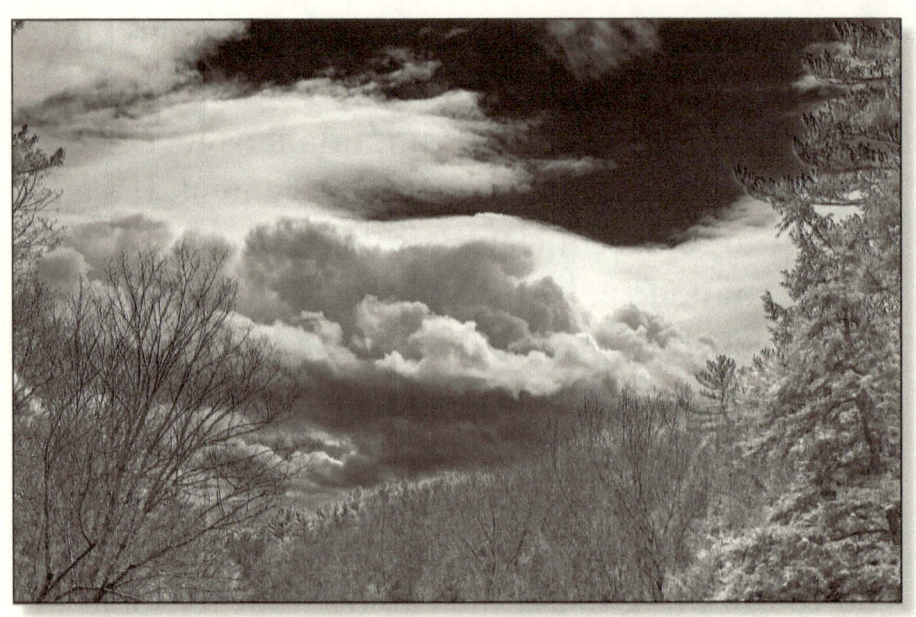

Saratoga Performing Arts Center, Saratoga Springs, N.Y., May 3, 2014.
Canon EOS 20D, 28 mm (44.2 mm), 1/800, f/16, ISO 400, P, pattern.
© 2015 by Shawn M. Tomlinson

ly quickly.

You start to attach the camera strap and after swearing at it for 15 minutes, you finally get it set.

You're ready.

Not really.

It would be a good time to read the manual...

No, you probably didn't get one with the camera, but not to worry. Canon still provides a free PDF download of the 20D manual (as of this writing) at http://gdlp01.c-wss.com/gds/9/0900000259/01/EOS20DIM-EN.pdf.

I realize most people don't read the manuals, and that includes me. I generally use them as references when I get stuck on something. The exception is my Nikon D1 which has such esoteric and complicated controls that it would be unlikely that I would ever memorize all of them.

So, yes, OK, you aren't going to read the manual, so I'll give you a few starting points for when the

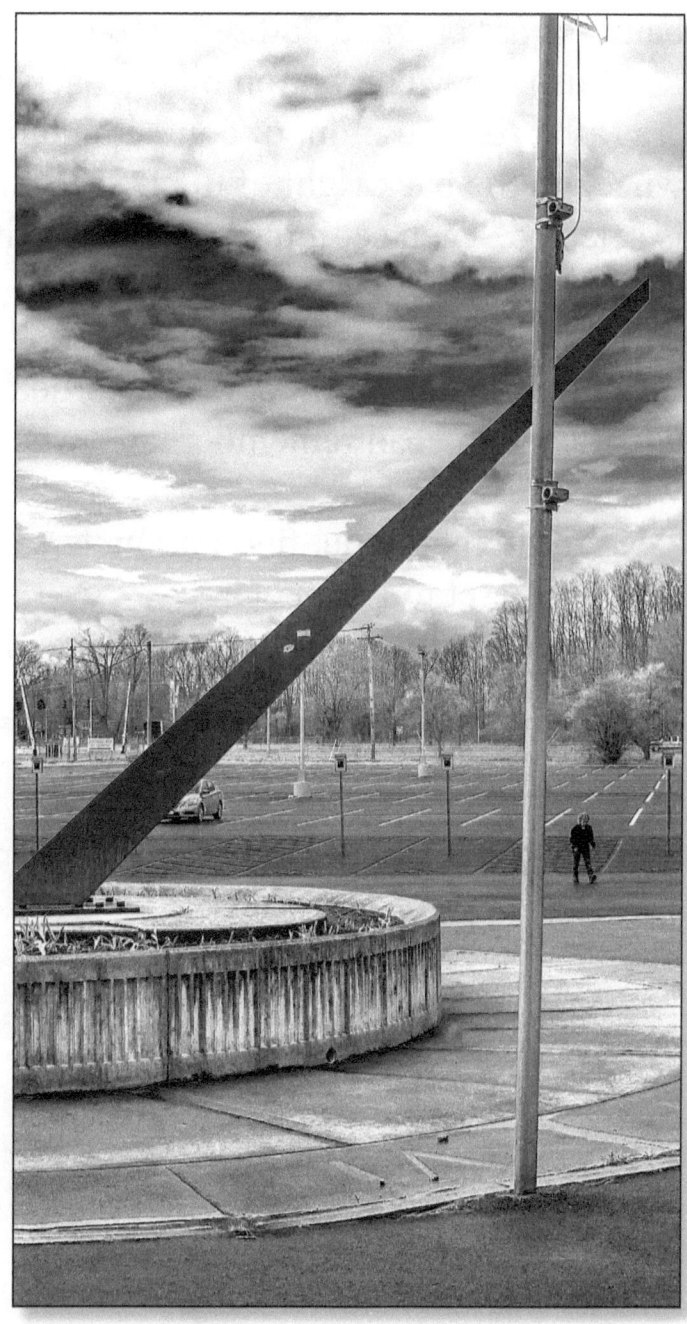

Saratoga Performing Arts Center, Saratoga Springs, N.Y., May 3, 2014. Canon EOS 20D, 30 mm (48 mm), 1/500, f/14, ISO 400, P, pattern.
© 2015 by Shawn M. Tomlinson

batteries are charged and ready to go.

• Push the Menu button on the back of the camera (after turning it on, of course) and rotate the big wheel on the back right of the DSLR until Quality is selected. Then set it to RAW in case it isn't there already.

• While we're in the Menus, set the Date/Time to the current date and time. It is recorded in each image file so you can remember later when you shot what.

• Still in the Menu, find Parameters and make certain it's set to Parameter 1.

• Go to the top right LCD screen and just above

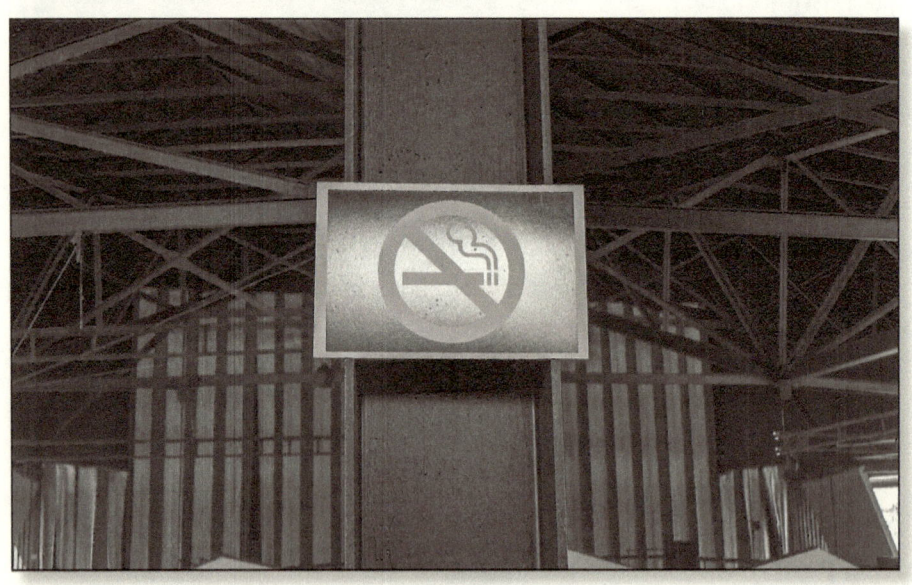

Saratoga Performing Arts Center, Saratoga Springs, N.Y., May 3, 2014.
Canon EOS 20D, 28 mm (44.2 mm), 1/80, f/5, ISO 400, P, pattern.
© 2015 by Shawn M. Tomlinson

it you'll find a button labeled "Drive/ISO." Press this and rotate the rear big wheel until it says "200" unless it's cloudy, then "400."

• Go to the top left of the 20D to the Mode dial. If this is your first time using a DSLR, set it to P (Program Mode). Note that this produces good, balanced images, but think of it like training wheels on a bicycle. As you learn to use the camera better, you will take the training wheels off and move to Tv (Shutter-Priority Mode) or Av (Aperture-Priority Mode) before taking the big plunge to the ultimate goal of M (Manual Mode).

• Look at the front of the camera to make certain

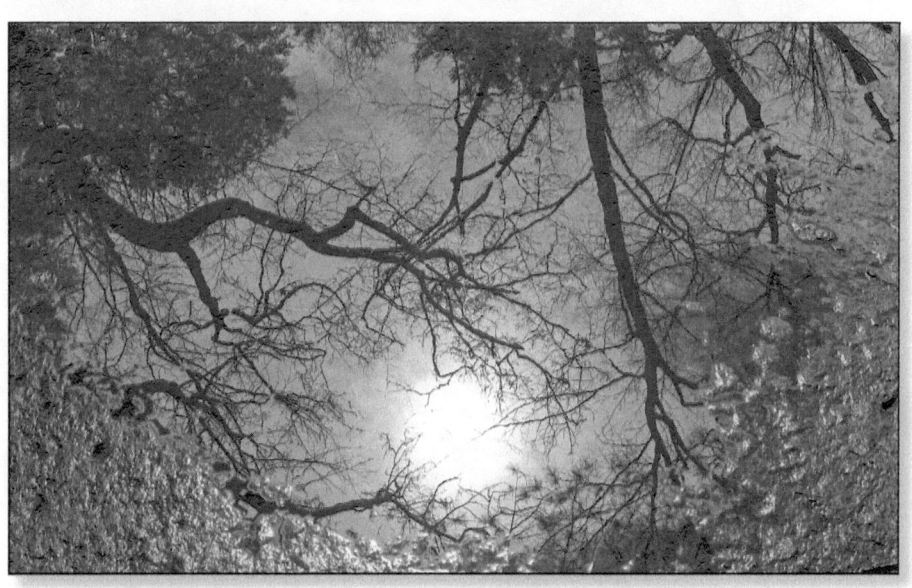

Saratoga Performing Arts Center, Saratoga Springs, N.Y., May 3, 2014.
Canon EOS 20D, 28 mm (44.2 mm), 1/400, f/11, ISO 400, P, pattern.
© 2015 by Shawn M. Tomlinson

the focus selector is set to AF (autofocus) unless you prefer M (manual focus).

A note here about why I include the battery grip as a main component of the 20D. Some people don't like grips because they increase the bulk and weight of cameras. True enough. They also give you double the battery power and a vertical shutter release button useful when you turn the DSLR vertical to shoot. Plus, at least for the 20D, a battery grip is really cheap, usually between $10 and $20.

So then, you've set up the camera.

Now you're ready.

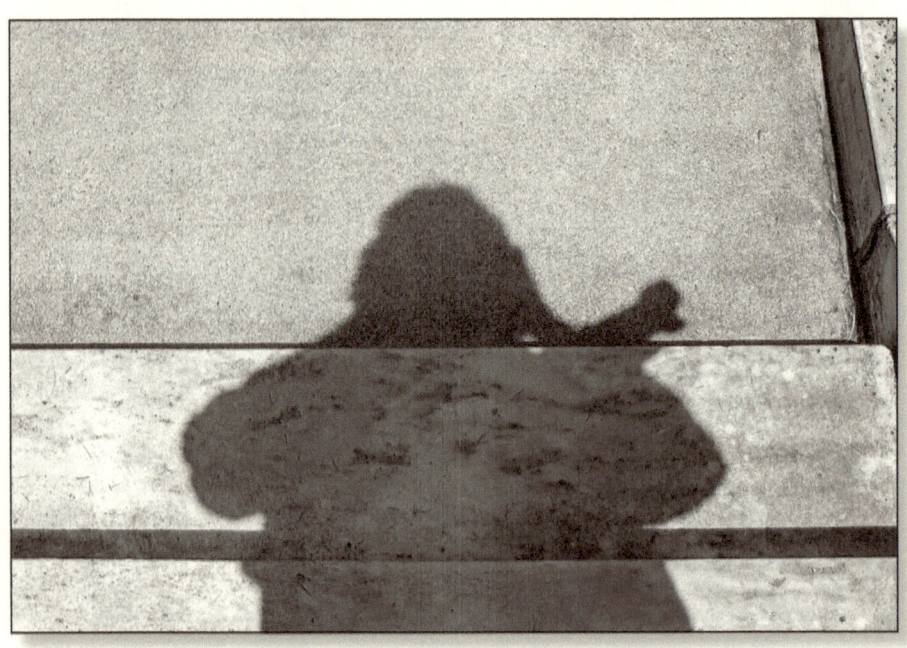

Shawn Tomlinson, Yaddo, Saratoga Springs, NY, May 10, 2014
Canon EOS 20D, 28mm, 1/250, f/9, ISO 200, P, pattern metering
© 2014, 2015 by Shawn M. Tomlinson

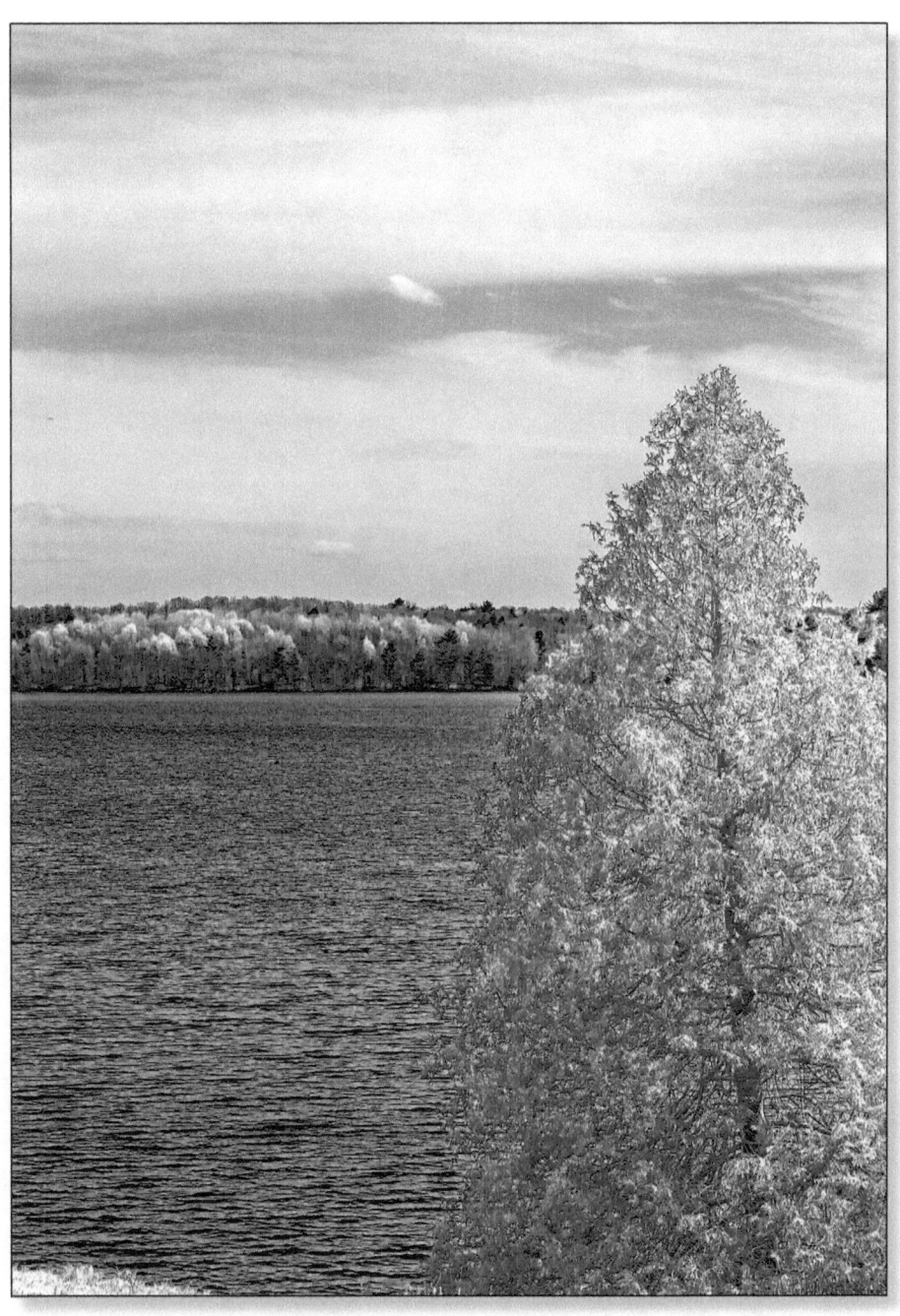

Galway Lake, Galway, NY, May 8, 2014
Canon EOS 20D, 58mm, 1/320, f/11, ISO 200, P, pattern metering
© 2014, 2015 by Shawn M. Tomlinson

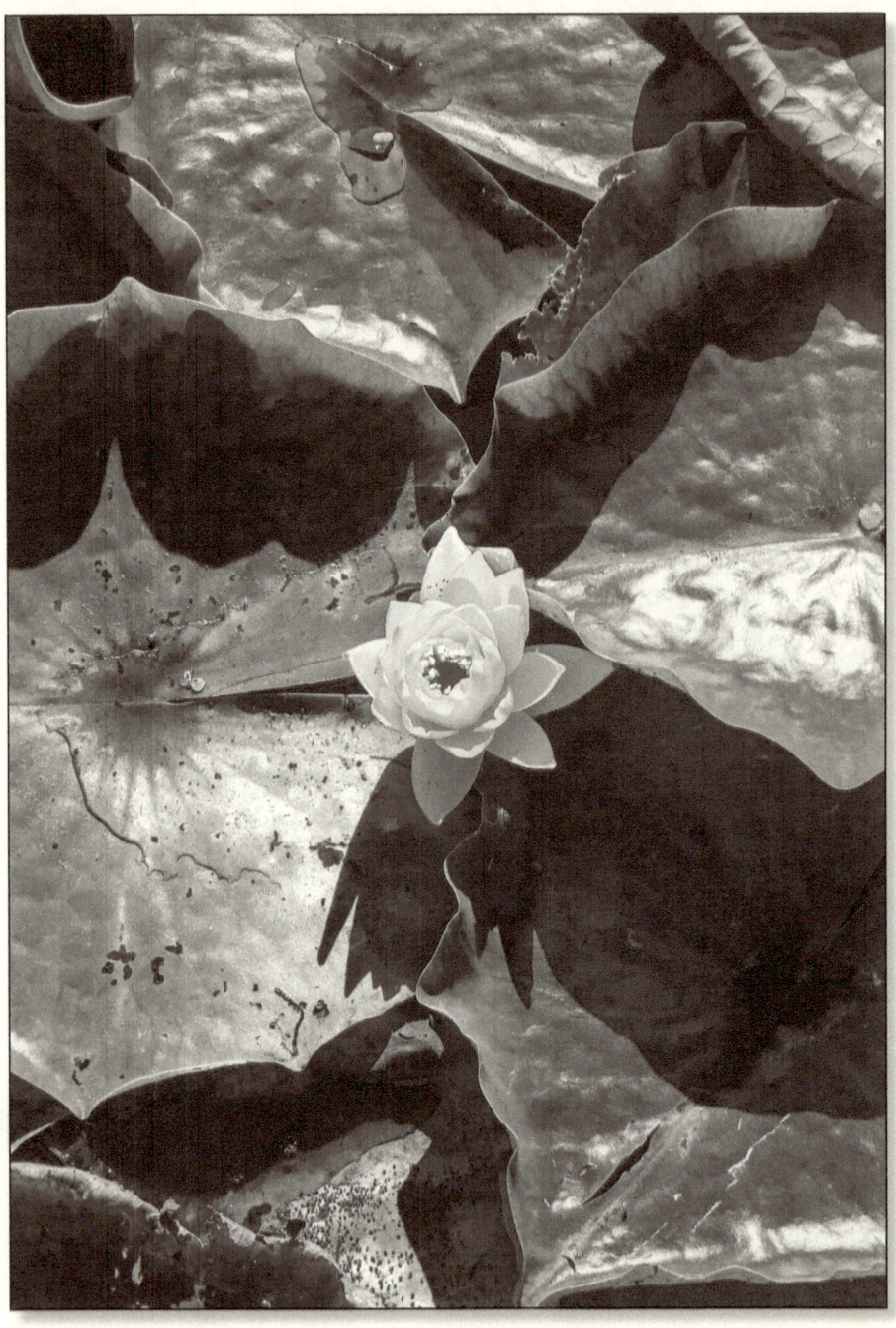

Ballston Lake, N.Y., July 11, 2014.
Canon EOS 20D, 80 mm (128 mm), 1/1250, f/5.6, ISO 200, Tv, pattern.
© 2015 by Shawn M. Tomlinson

Part 4
Exploring With the 20D

No matter how experienced you are, it's never a good idea to take a new-to-you DSLR on an important and/or paying job.

It will slow you down because you don't know where all the controls are, and you just got an old, used camera. If you bought it from a reputable photographic equipment dealer such as KEH (which I can personally recommend and do), chances are the DSLR will work fine. If you bought it from eBay or Goodwill Auctions or some other place, it may not.

The best idea with any new camera, especially an old one, is to get out and shoot at least a few sessions before taking it into a serious assignment.

I always recommend shooting in one's own backyard or neighborhood. It's close, it's familiar and it gives you a chance to really "see" things as photographic subjects you may never have noticed previously.

Wait, you have wildflowers growing in the backyard? Hmmm. Wait, you have a playful rottweiler standing there looking at you with her bright yellow plastic pig in her mouth? Again, hmmm. Wait, you have kids playing on a swing set?

Well, you get the idea.

Don't just shoot these subjects like snapshots, either. Think of them as a photo assignment and really *look* at them. See them from different, unusual angles. Get really close to those wildflowers, as close as the lens will focus. See that blurry background? That's called bokeh and when shot well, gives great images. It makes the main subject stand out well.

Once you get familiar enough with the 20D to feel confident, head out to some of your favorite

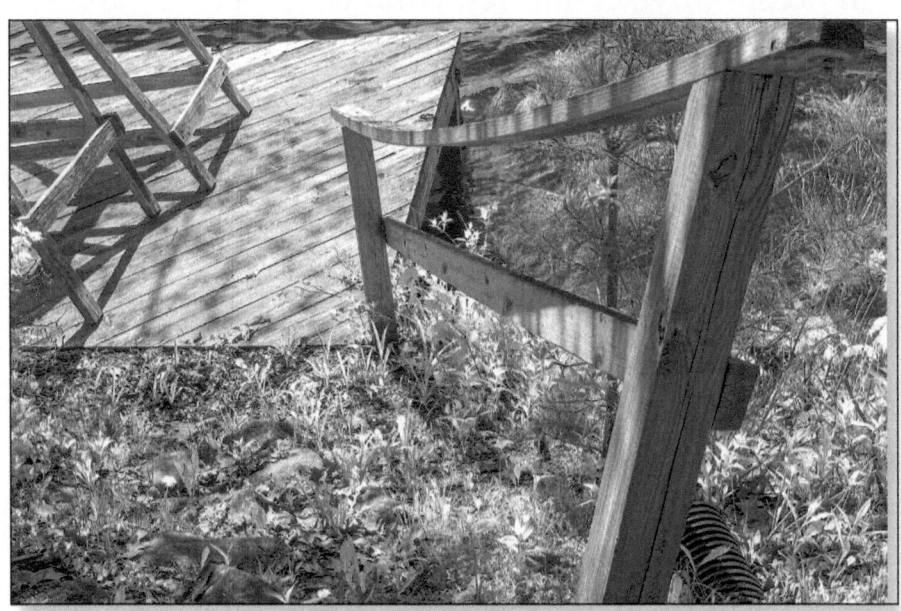

West Lake, N.Y., May 21, 2014.
Canon EOS 20D, 28 mm (44.2 mm), 1/60, f/11, ISO 200, A-DEP, pattern.
© 2015 by Shawn M. Tomlinson

photographic locations. If you bought the camera to use as a backup or second DSLR, be brave and make your voyage of photography with *only* the 20D. Force yourself to rely upon it — for non-paying jobs — and explore. This makes it necessary for you to really get to know the camera and its capabilities, and to push it to its limits. You will be amazed at the results.

I make a conscious choice every day — I shoot every day — about which camera I will use for each photo session. I have the gadget bag with me with a second and sometimes third DSLR waiting, but I leave them in the car while I go shooting. The

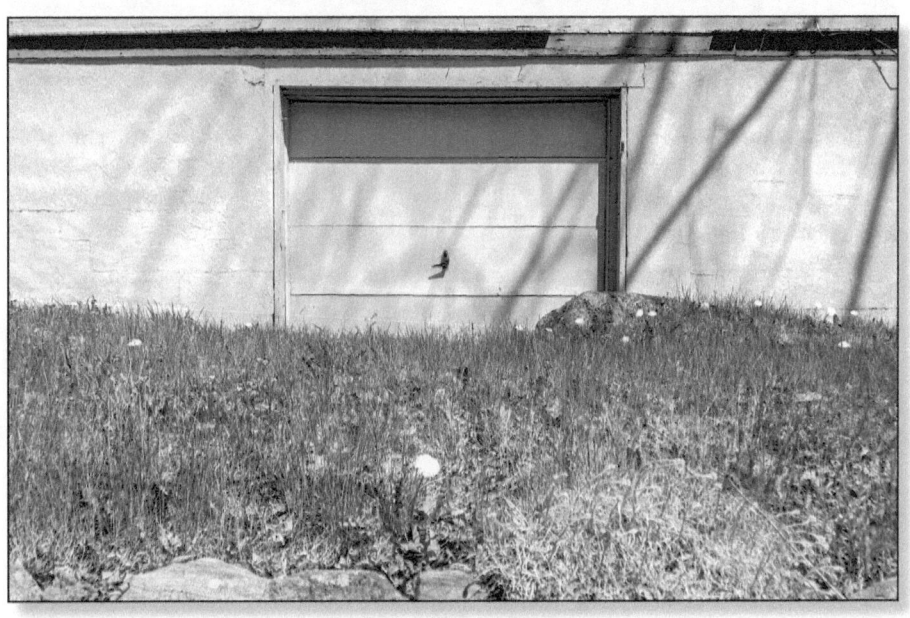

West Lake, N.Y., May 21, 2014.
Canon EOS 20D, 28 mm (44.2 mm), 1/1000, f/5, ISO 200, Tv, pattern.
© 2015 by Shawn M. Tomlinson

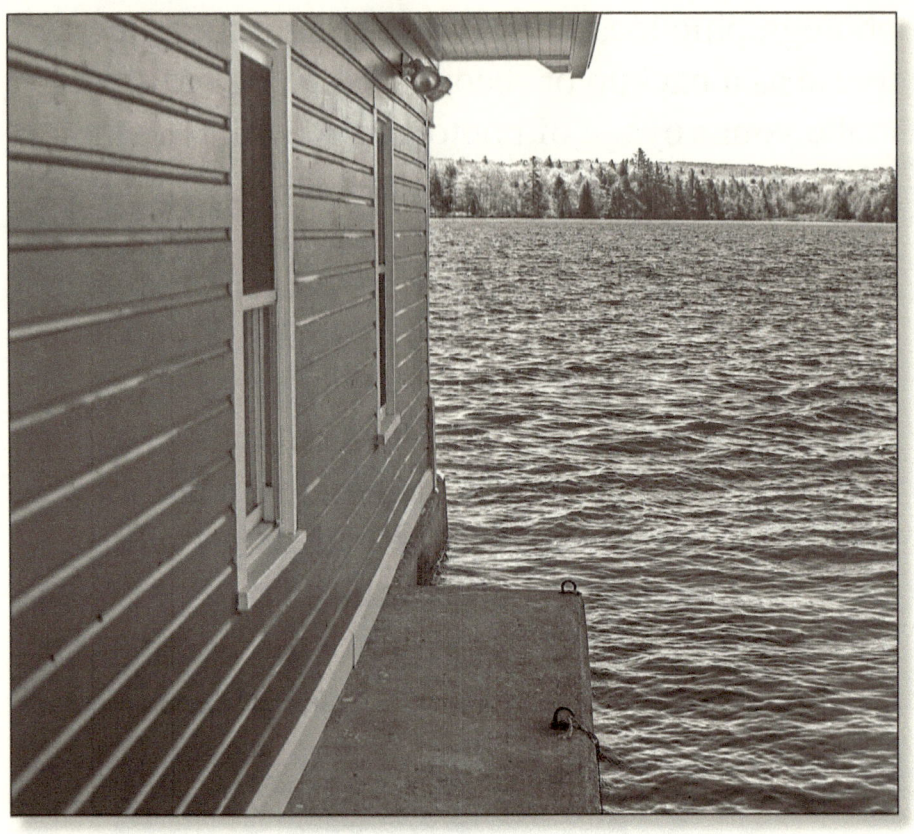

West Lake, N.Y., May 21, 2014.
Canon EOS 20D, 28 mm (44.2 mm), 1/1000, f/3.5, ISO 200, A-DEP, pattern.
© 2015 by Shawn M. Tomlinson

decision comes down to two things, usually: what kind of color am I looking for today and which camera appeals to me today?

When the 20D first arrived, I shot almost exclusively with it for about a month. I wanted to see what it did in every circumstance I could concoct. It never let me down. Now when I don't use it as often, it astounds me even more when I do shoot with it. When I put that CF card in the reader and copy the image files to the hard drive, I'm not necessarily thinking, "Ooo, these are going to be great." But when I open the folder in Adobe Bridge and start looking at them, it is then that I am astounded.

I shoot with Nikon DSLRs most of the time, and they certainly produce great color and sharp images. Yet, when I shoot with the 20D, I see a difference in the color. It's warmer, more inviting. Every time I shoot with the 20D, I start thinking, "Ya know, maybe the next DSLR should be a newer Canon." And it may be be when I go to my next to

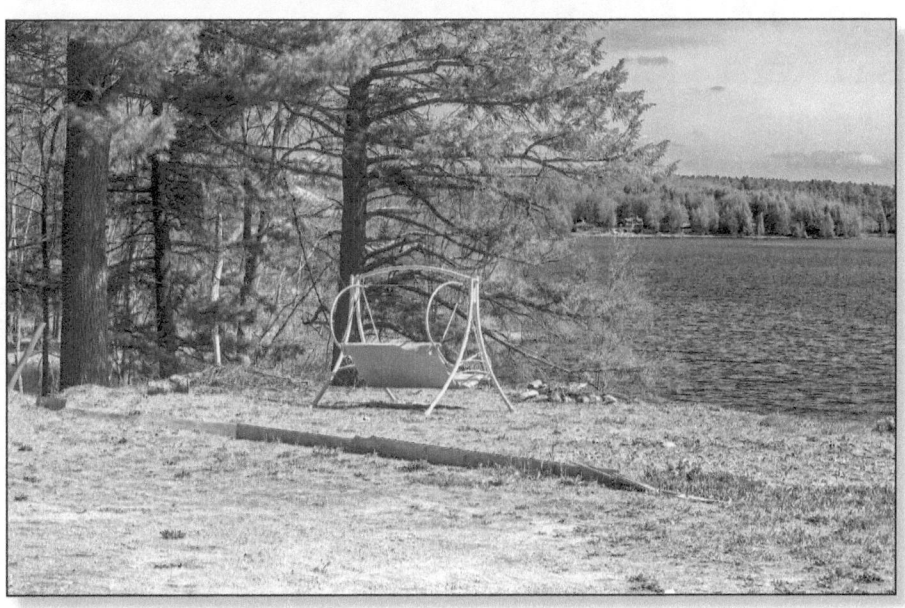

Galway Lake, N.Y., May 8, 2014.
Canon EOS 20D, 53 mm (84.8 mm), 1/320, f/11, ISO 200, P, pattern.
© 2015 by Shawn M. Tomlinson

full-frame camera.

I did shoot with a full-frame Canon EOS 1DS for a time and was fairly impressed except that that particular camera had sensor problems, so I sent it back and replaced it with a Nikon. I would have replaced it with another 1DS, but one of the downsides of buying used pho-

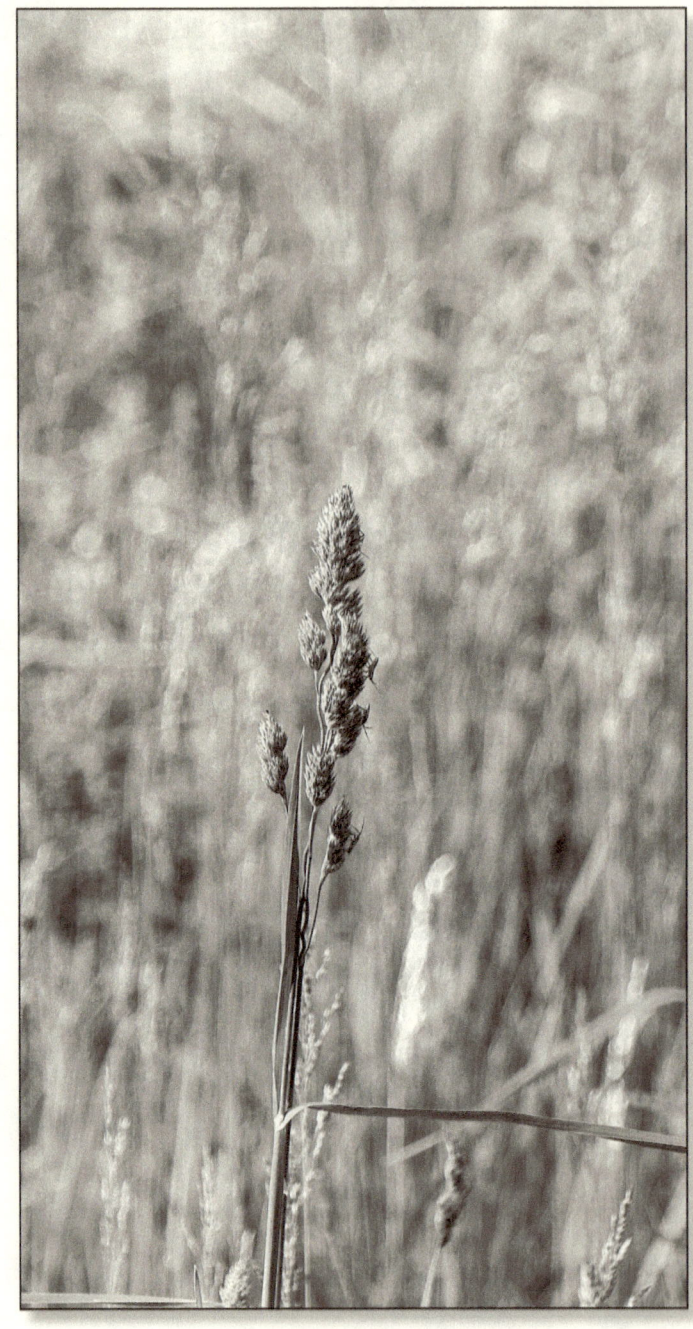

Rotterdam Junction, N.Y., May 27, 2014.
Canon EOS 20D, 149 mm (238.4 mm), 1/250, f/5.6, ISO 200, P, pattern.
© 2015 by Shawn M. Tomlinson

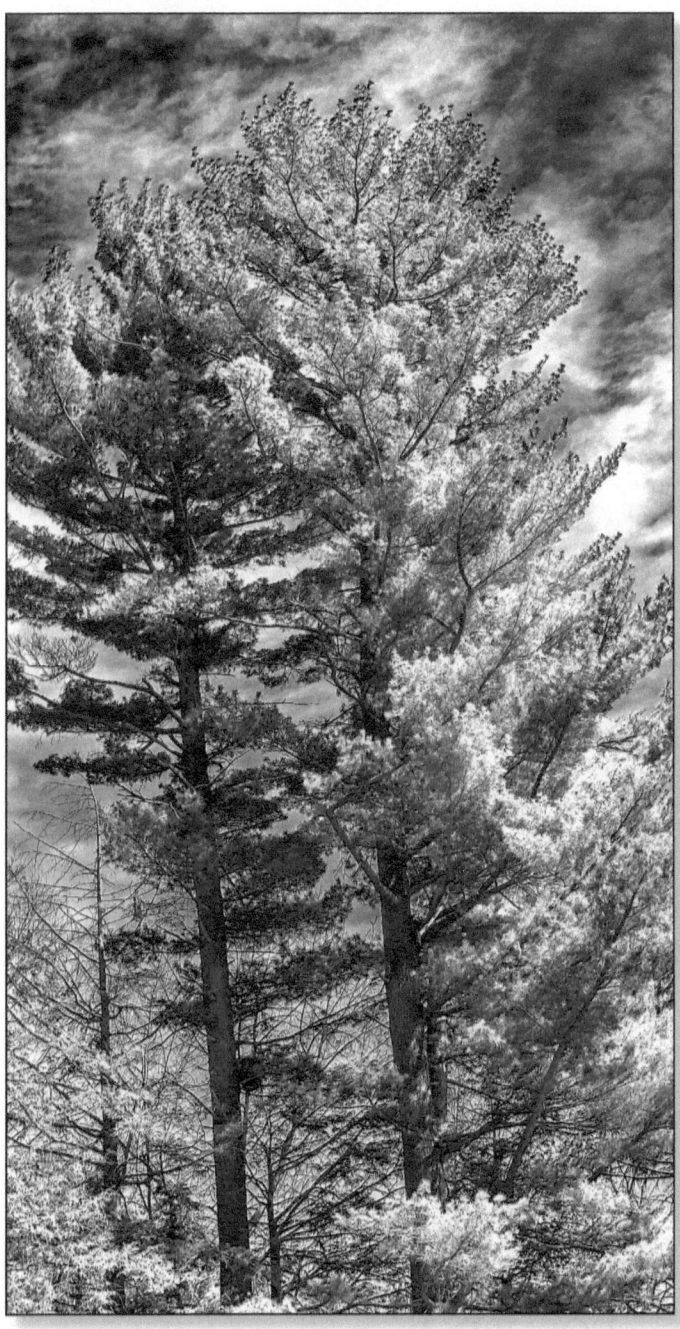

tographic equipment is that re-sellers only have what they have in stock. At the time, KEH did not have another 1DS, but it did have a price-dropped Nikon D7000, so I delayed full frame in favor of the much-lauded D7000.

Older Canon full-frame DSLRs also tend to be cheaper

Galway Lake, N.Y., May 8, 2014.
Canon EOS 20D, 28 mm (44.2 mm), 1/250, f/10, ISO 200, P, pattern.
© 2015 by Shawn M. Tomlinson

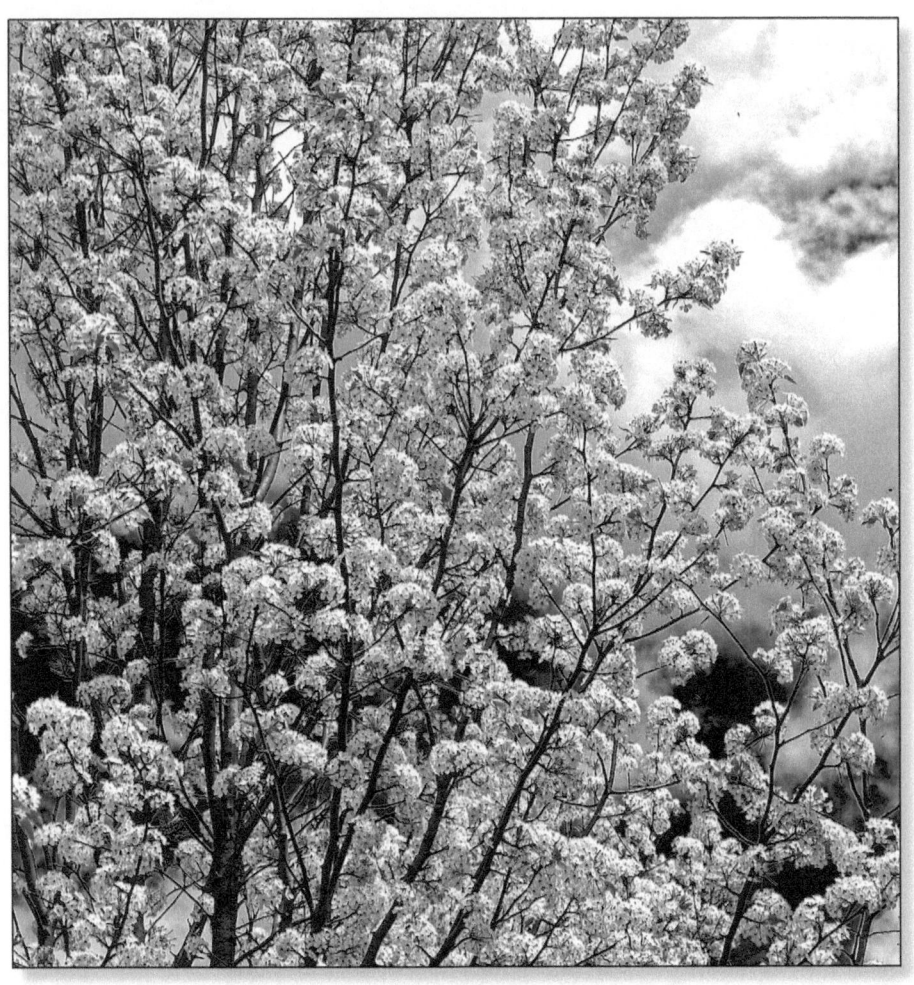

Saratoga Springs, N.Y., May 10, 2014.
Canon EOS 20D, 65 mm (104 mm), 1/320, f/11, ISO 200, P, pattern.
© 2015 by Shawn M. Tomlinson

than Nikons, so that is yet another incentive to stick with Canon for that move.

If you are planning eventually to go to full frame from the Canon EOS 20D, keep in mind that any lenses you buy should be EF and not EF-S. EF-S lenses will work on Canon's APS-C or crop-frame sensor DSLRs, but they will not mount on Canon's full frame cameras. So, if you choose an 18-55mm "kit" lens to go with the 20D, fine, it's a good enough lens. Just keep in mind you will need to keep using it with the 20D — or 30D, 40D, 70D, etc. — and not on a Canon EOS 5D, 6D or 1DS models. You will need different lenses. Now, if you choose to go with a prime lens, say a 50mm or 28mm for the 20D — which is a great idea — then you have no worries. These lenses only are made in the EF mount and will work wonderfully on a full-frame camera as well as the 20D.

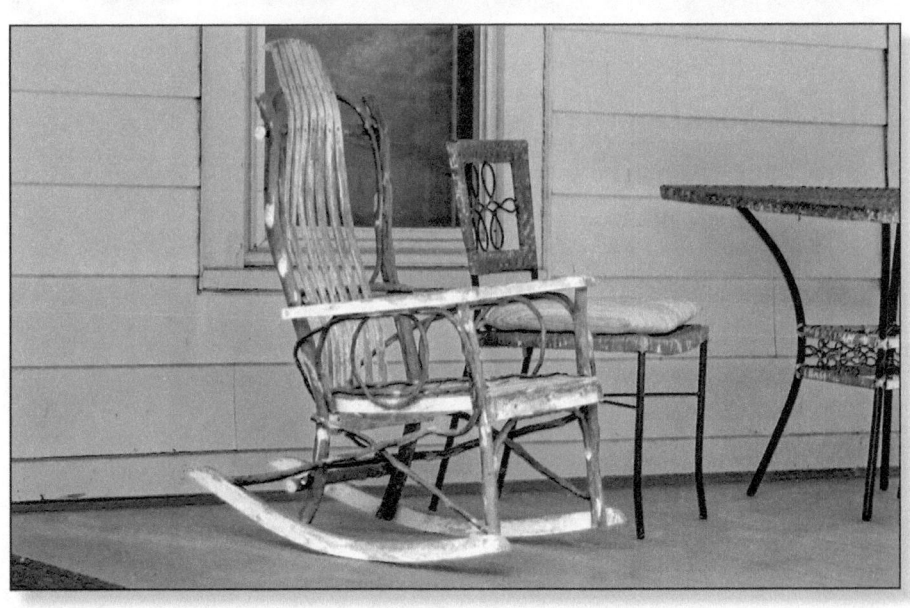

Saratoga Springs, NY, June 3, 2014
Canon EOS 20D, 80mm, 1/60, f/5.6, ISO 200, P, pattern metering
© 2014, 2015 by Shawn M. Tomlinson

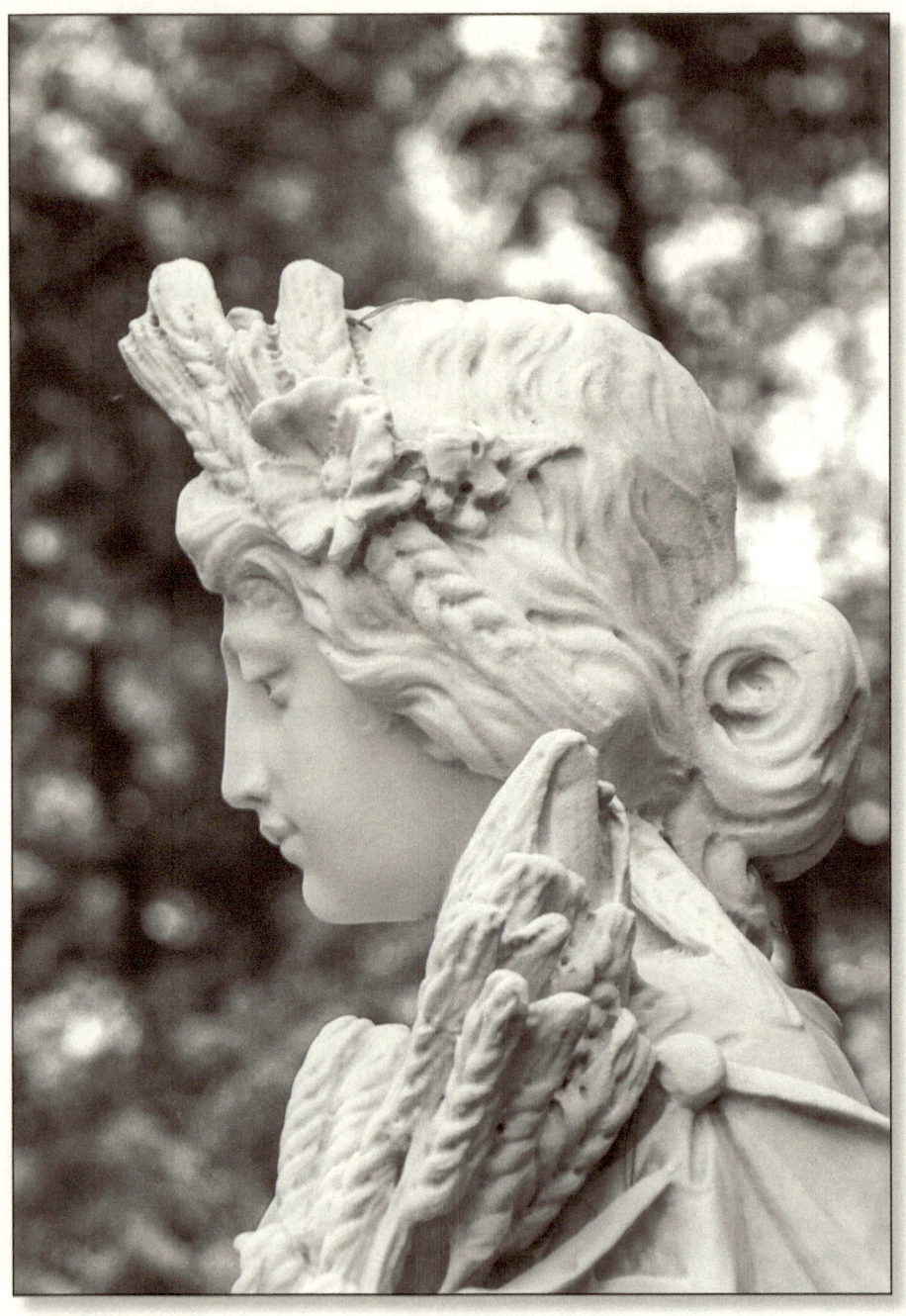

Yaddo, Saratoga Springs, NY, May 10, 2014
Canon EOS 20D, 200mm, 1/60, f/10, ISO 100, Av, pattern metering
© 2014, 2015 by Shawn M. Tomlinson

Part 5
Where to Go
From Here

If the Canon EOS 20D is your second or third DSLR, then you already know what to do next to keep exploring the camera's capabilities. If it's your first, here are some ideas.

• Get some other lenses.

Aside from better technology and picture quality, one of the main advantages of a DSLR is the ability to use a variety of lenses on one camera body. Not at the same time, of course. There are so many, though, what to choose?

The most basic setup that will cover a lot of photographic possibilities without breaking the bank is:

A) One prime lens: 24mm, 28mm, 35mm, 50mm, 85mm or 100mm. You probably don't need more than one of these, but you do need one. Unless, of course, you are like me and mostly shoot with primes. Prime lenses only have one focal length, but they typically are sharper and brighter than zoom lenses. Keep in mind that Canon APS-C cameras have a 1.6x focal length modifier because of the sensor size. Lens makers still use the old

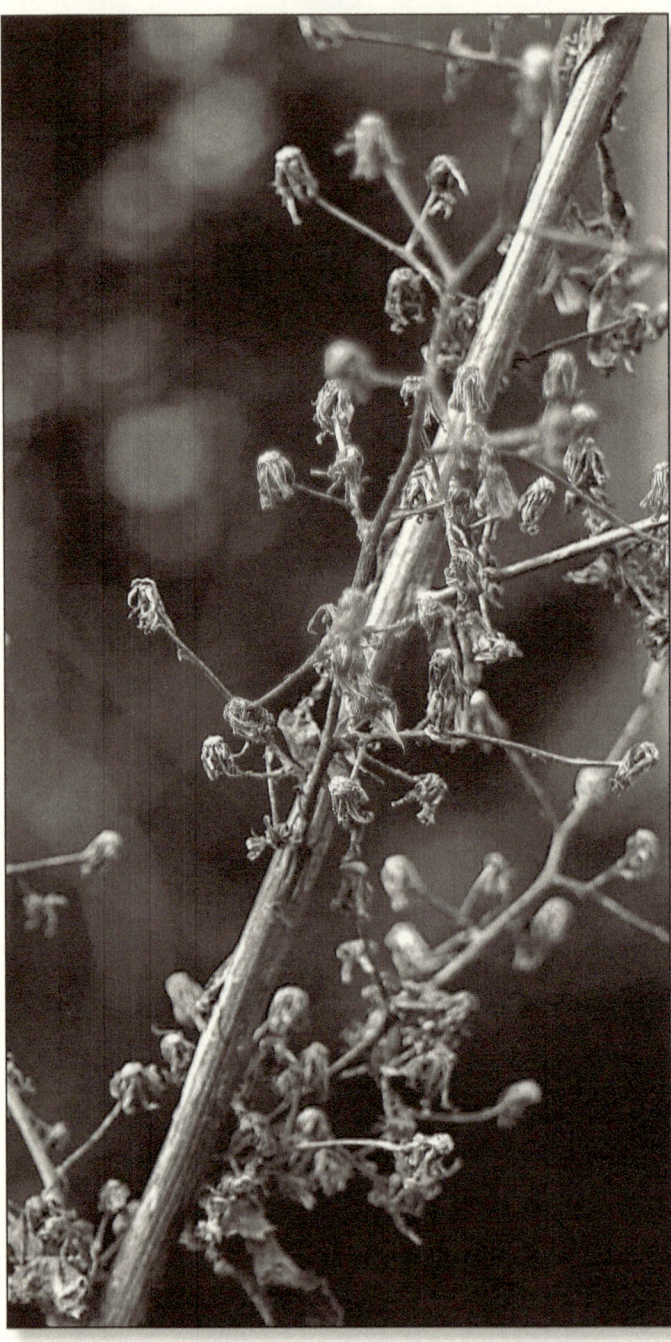

Ballston Lake, N.Y., May 6, 2014.
Canon EOS 20D, 80 mm (128 mm), 1/100, f/5.6, ISO 200, P, pattern.
© 2015 by Shawn M. Tomlinson

35mm film focal length designations for lenses, even those made only for APS-C cameras. Where the 24mm lens used to be about the widest angle lens you could get without the fisheye effect beginning to appear, on an APS-C Canon camera, it is the equivalent of 38.4mm, so it no longer is that wide. The 1.6x factor makes these prime lenses effectively:

24mm = 38.4mm

28mm = 44.8mm

35mm = 56mm

50mm = 80mm

85mm = 136mm

100mm = 160mm

They're still all very useful for different things, just not as wide as they would

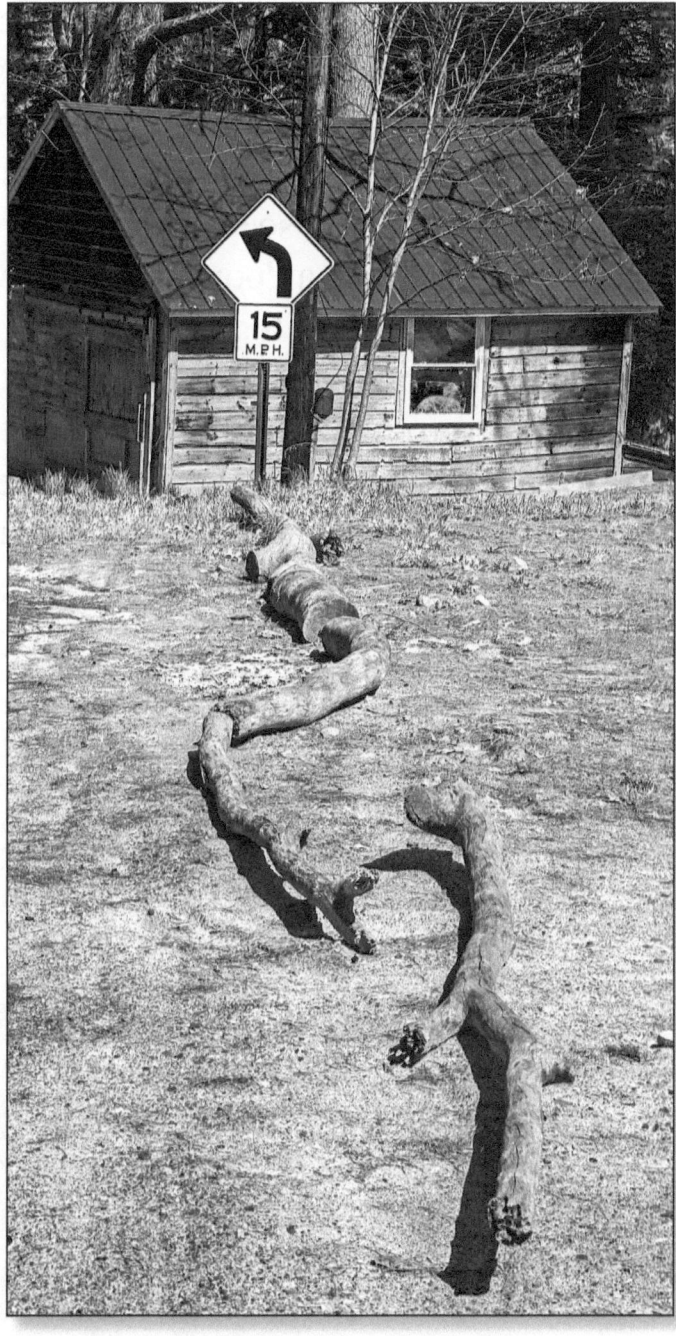

Galway Lake, N.Y., May 8, 2014.
Canon EOS 20D, 42 mm (67.2 mm), 1/400, f/11, ISO 200, P, pattern.
© 2015 by Shawn M. Tomlinson

be on a full-frame camera. The 24mm and 28mm will give you slightly wide-angle angles of view; the 35mm now is classified as a "normal" lens meaning that what you see through it is about the same size as how you see with your eyes alone; The 50mm lens becomes a "portrait" lens, which means it gives great bokeh to highlight your subject; The 85mm and 100mm are short telephotos, also great for portraits producing even better bokeh.

If you were going to get two of these prime lenses, it would make sense to get one from either end, a 24mm and an 85mm. If you're only getting one, well, I prefer the 50mm. It's produces great bokeh

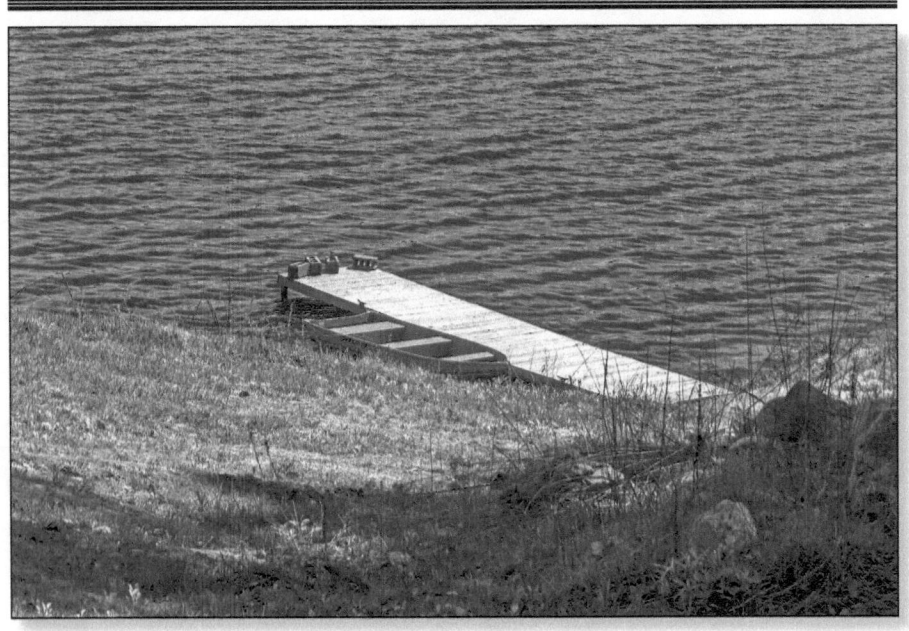

Galway Lake, N.Y., May 8, 2014.
Canon EOS 20D, 80 mm (128 mm), 1/400, f/11, ISO 200, P, pattern.
© 2015 by Shawn M. Tomlinson

and it's not that expensive. I also like the 35mm and 28mm, but I have yet to purchase either.

B) One zoom lens: The most flexible zoom lens is an 18-200mm "travel" lens. It covers the equivalent of 28.8mm to 320mm. It is not as sharp or free of distortion or chromatic aberration as shorter, better built zooms, but that's the trade off for the extra range. It's a great starter lens for the 20D camera, and as long as you don't need razor sharp images, it will serve you well.

The better the lens, though, the better the images. Better lenses even on older DSLRs produce better images.

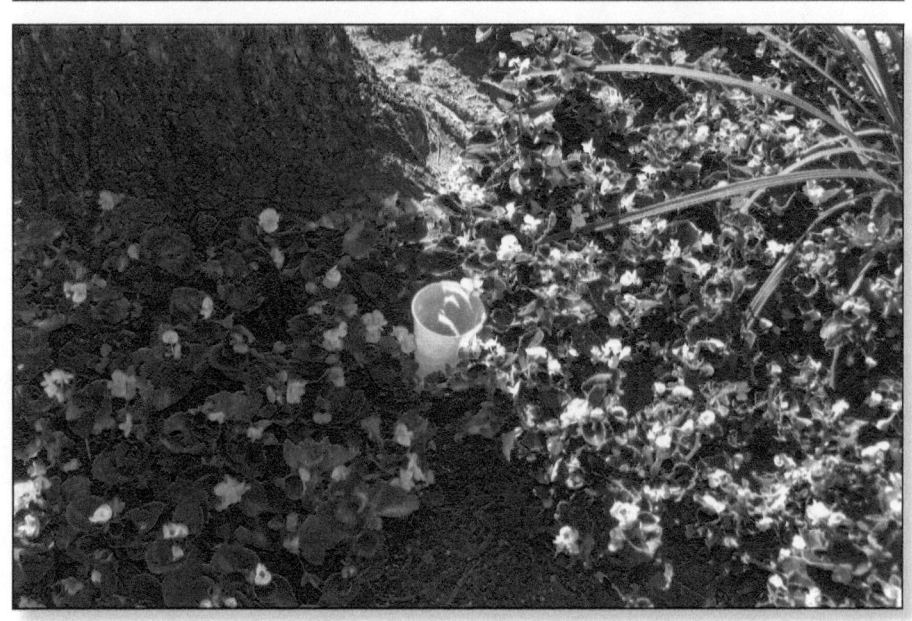

Saratoga Springs, N.Y., Aug. 19, 2014.
Canon EOS 20D, 28 mm (44.2 mm), 1/2500, f/3.5, ISO 400, Tv, pattern.
© 2015 by Shawn M. Tomlinson

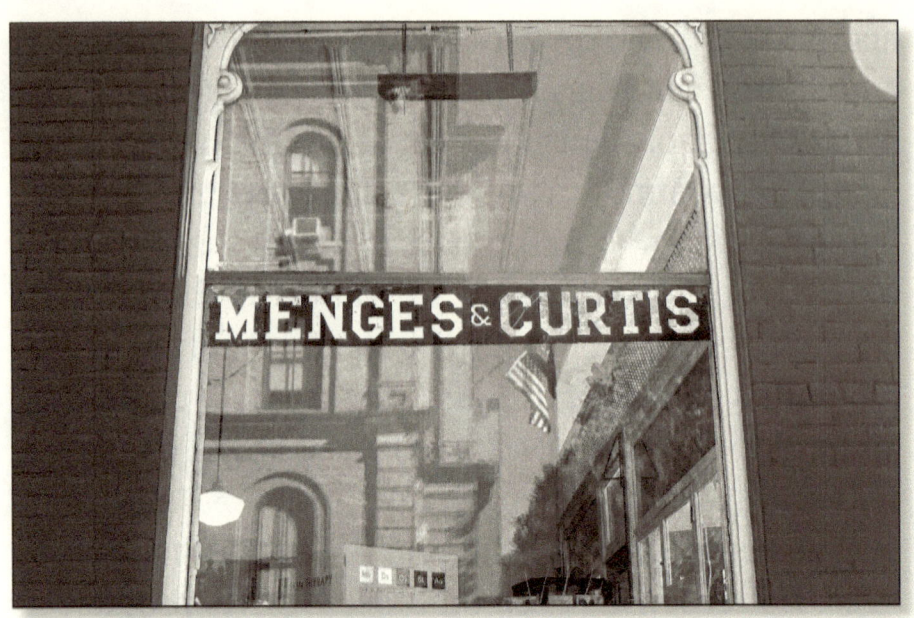

Saratoga Springs, N.Y., Aug. 19, 2014.
Canon EOS 20D, 28 mm (44.2 mm), 1/2500, f/3.5, ISO 400, Tv, pattern.
© 2015 by Shawn M. Tomlinson

Canon's best lenses are designated with an "L" and a red ring around the lens barrel. The two most useful of these are the Canon EF L 17-40mm and the Canon EF L 24-105mm. These, even used, will cost many times more than other lenses and at least six times as much as the 20D itself costs used.

The least expensive choices for zoom lenses for the 20D are a 28-80mm former "kit" lens (sold originally with Canon film autofocus SLRs) and an 18-55mm "kit" lens (usually sold with entry-level DSLR cameras). The 28-80mm can be had very cheaply if you look on auction sites, not for the lens, but for autofocus film Canon cameras. I got

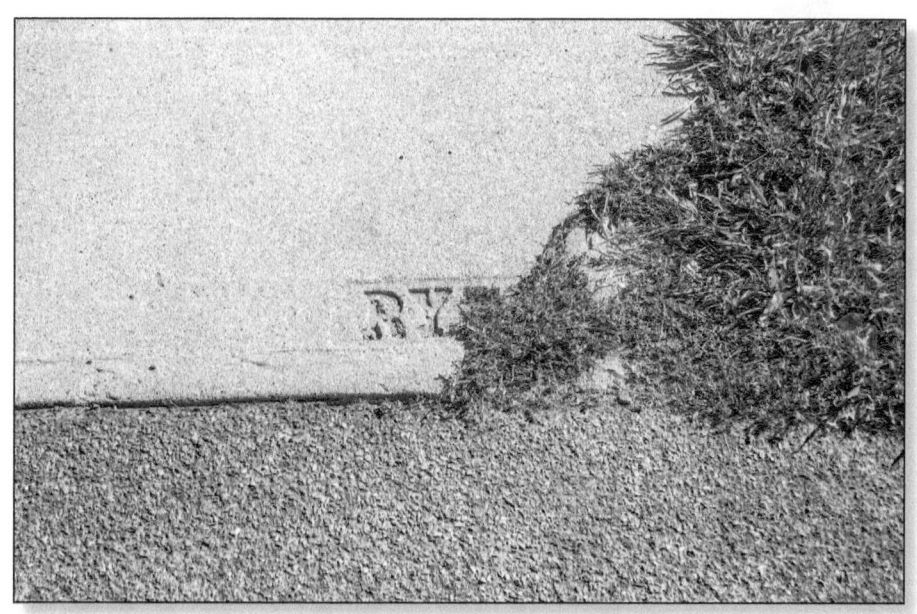

Saratoga Springs, N.Y., Aug. 19, 2014.
Canon EOS 20D, 35 mm (56 mm), 1/2500, f/5, ISO 400, Tv, pattern.
© 2015 by Shawn M. Tomlinson

mine attached to an early Rebel for $35. I've never used the Rebel, but I've used the lens often.

Kit lenses typically are not of the best optical quality, but they're still good. As long as you buy any lens made by Canon and not a third-party — Sigma, Tamron, Tokina or Velveeta (Quantaray; "Quantaray is to lenses as Velveeta is to cheese") — you will get a fast-focusing lens with fairly sharp detail.

• Get some other accessories.

A) Gadget bag. Chances are if you are relatively serious about photography, you will acquire more than one camera body. For this reason, it makes more sense to acquire a gadget bag that holds at least two camera bodies right at the start. These aren't cheap. A good Tamrac, for example, will cost as least as much as you paid for the 20D. You are protecting precious equipment, however, and if it means anything to you, you need a good gadget bag. I bought a Tamrac Pro 8 bag more than a decade ago. It has had a lot of use between my days working for newspapers to my later work as a solo photographer, and it shows very few signs of wear.

If you are really into protecting your gear, then a Zero Halliburton or Pelican case is worthwhile, if less convenient. I have my Hasselblad in a Pelican

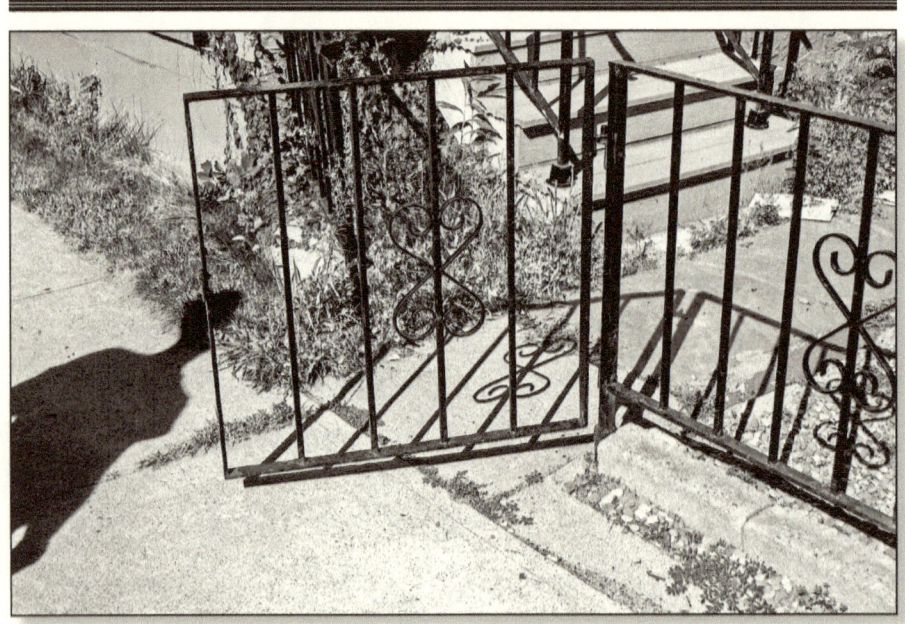

Gary W. Ziroli, Saratoga Springs, N.Y., Aug. 19, 2014.
Canon EOS 20D, 35 mm (56 mm), 1/2500, f/4.5, ISO 400, Tv, pattern.
© 2015 by Shawn M. Tomlinson

water-tight case, but I also don't use it much. When I did, getting it in and out of the case was time-consuming and frustrating.

These kinds of hard cases do offer much more protection that soft gadget bags, however, so many photographers swear by them.

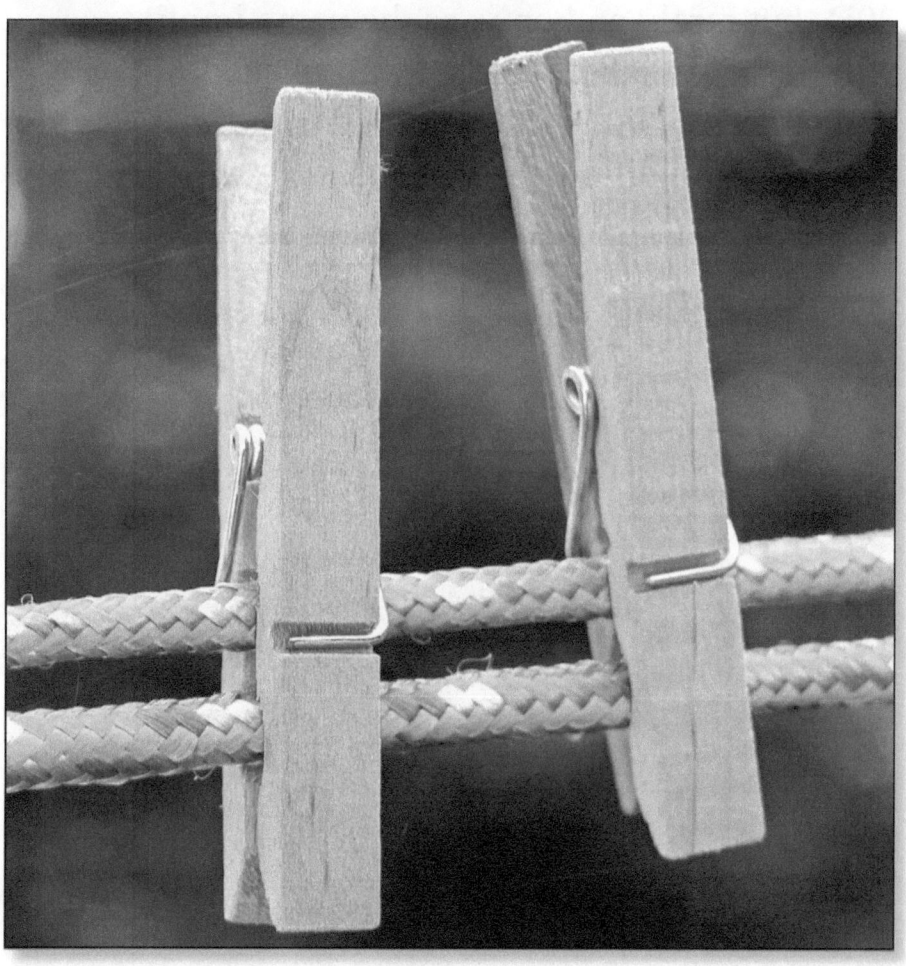

Ballston Lake, N.Y., Aug. 6, 2014.
Canon EOS 20D, 80 mm (128 mm), 1/200, f/8, ISO 400, P, pattern.
© 2015 by Shawn M. Tomlinson

I usually just swear at them.

B) Flash. I don't use external flash much, so here you are kind-of on your own. I do know from my earlier experience with Pentax that buying a flash made by the same company that made your camera offers advantages. It will cost a lot more, though. I do occasionally use the popup fill flash with my 20D, but rarely and only, as the name implies, as "fill flash." In other words, to fill in shadows or darker areas a little. The popup flash is not great for really good lighting.

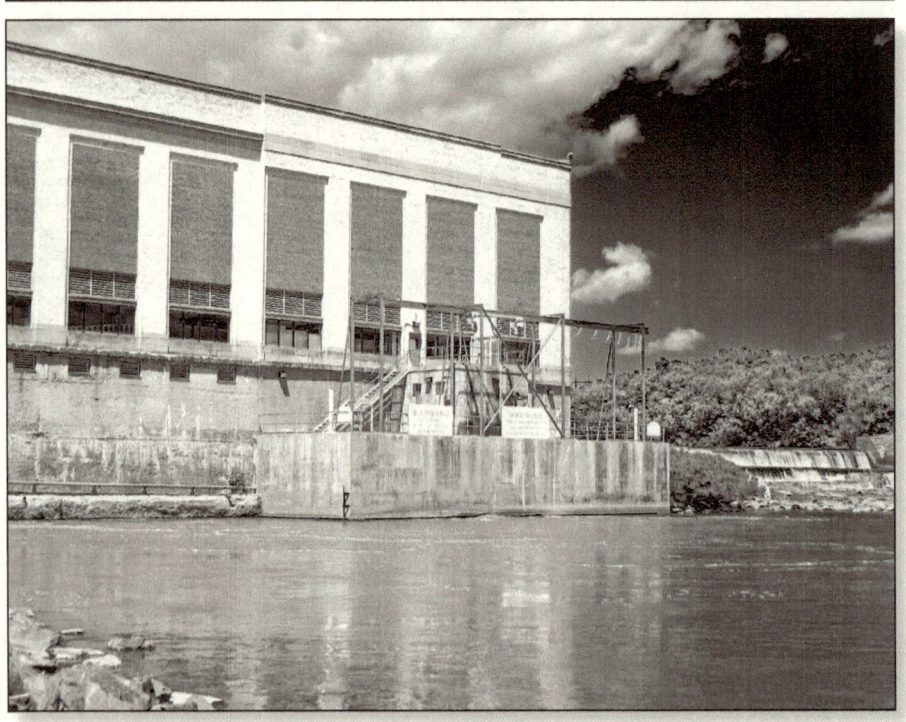

Cohoes, NY, June 7, 2014
Canon EOS 20D, 28mm, 1/2000, f/3.5, ISO 200, S, pattern metering
© 2014, 2015 by Shawn M. Tomlinson

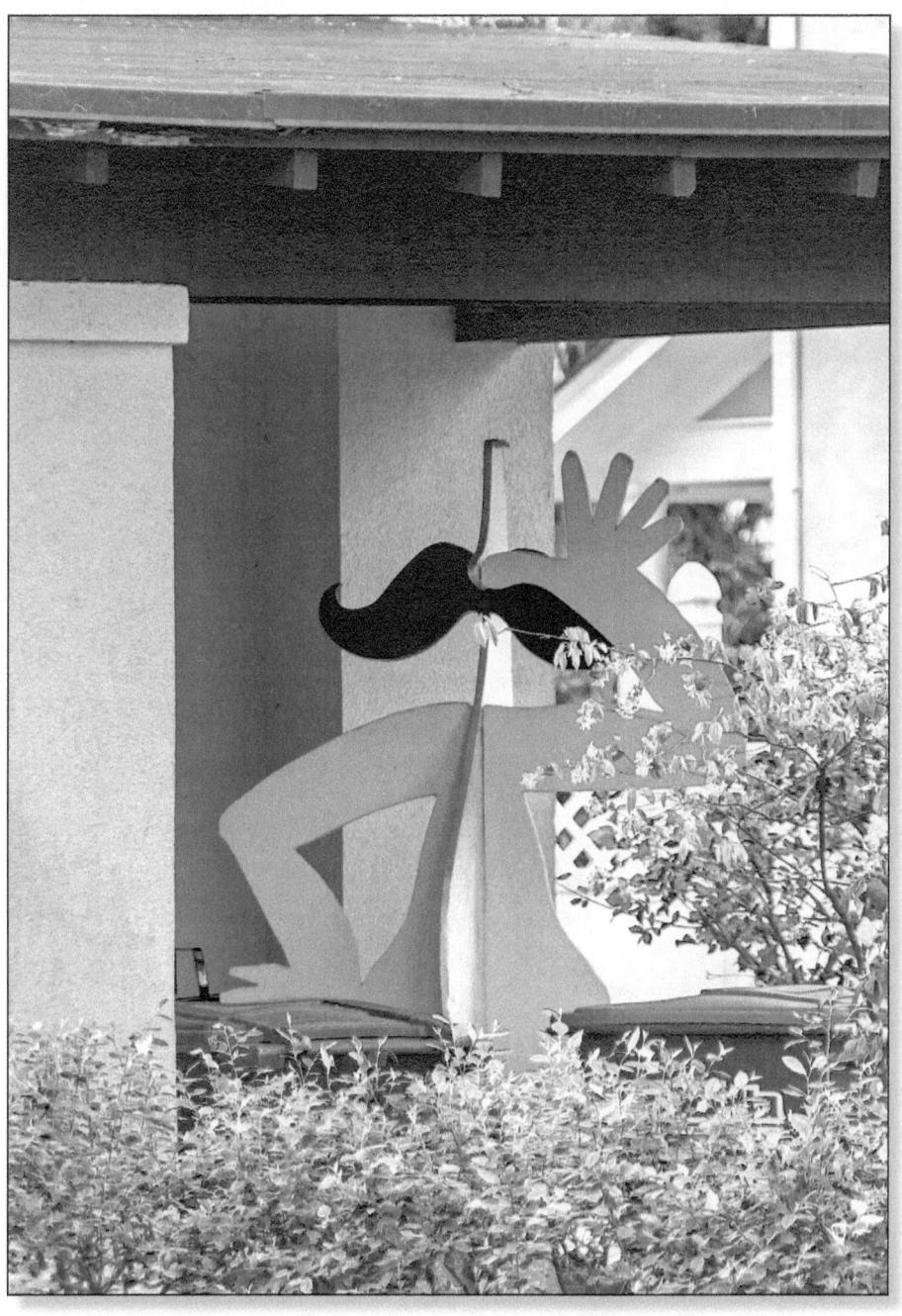

Saratoga Springs, NY, June 10, 2014
Canon EOS 20D, 200mm, 1/125, f/6.7, ISO 200, S, pattern metering
© 2014, 2015 by Shawn M. Tomlinson

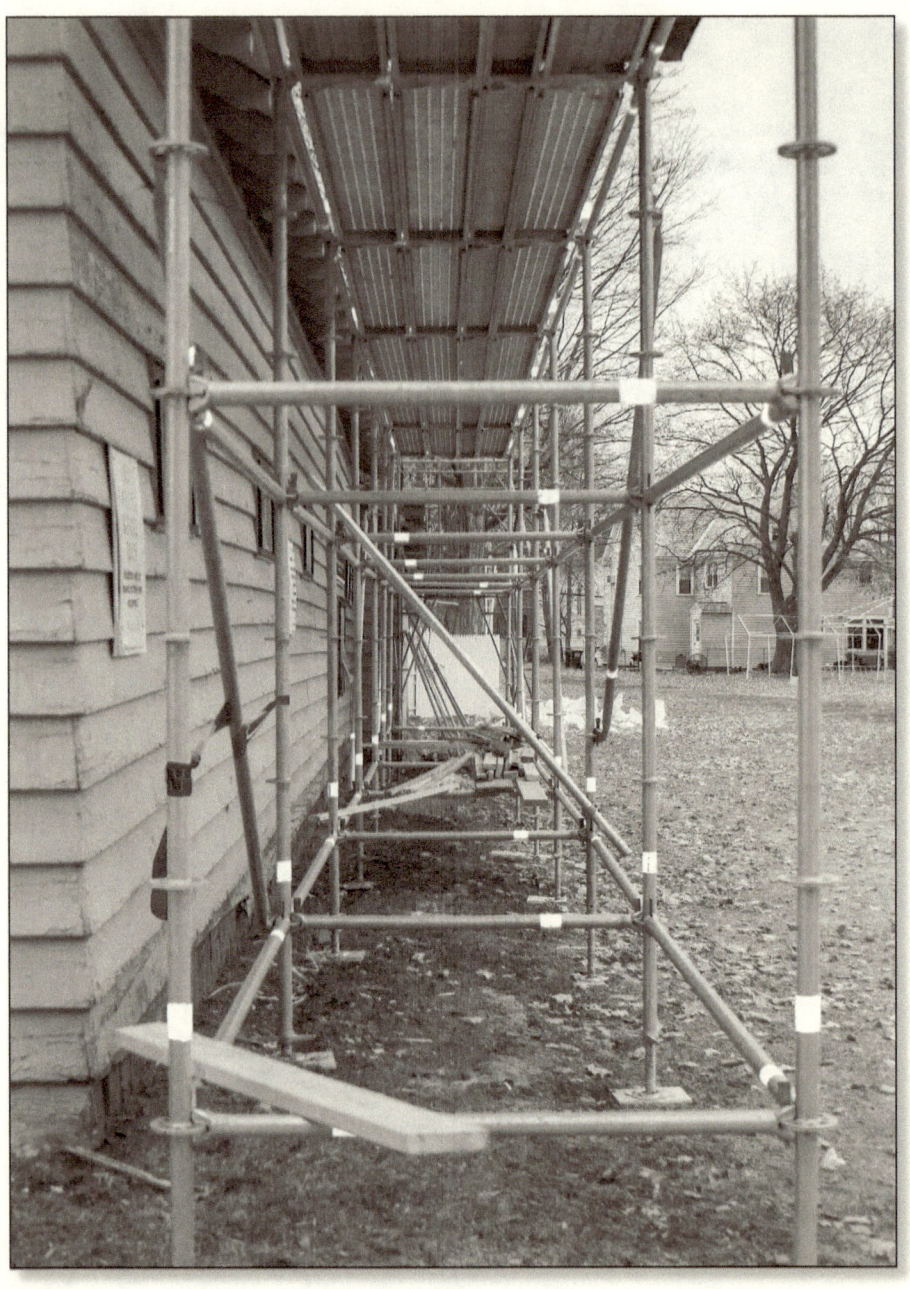

Saratoga Springs, N.Y., Jan. 3, 2015.
Canon EOS 20D, 28 mm (44.2 mm), 1/320, f/4.5, ISO 400, Tv, pattern.
© 2015 by Shawn M. Tomlinson

Last Words

As you probably can tell at this point, I really can't say enough good things about the Canon EOS 20D. And no, Canon does not compensate me in any way, and the company probably would

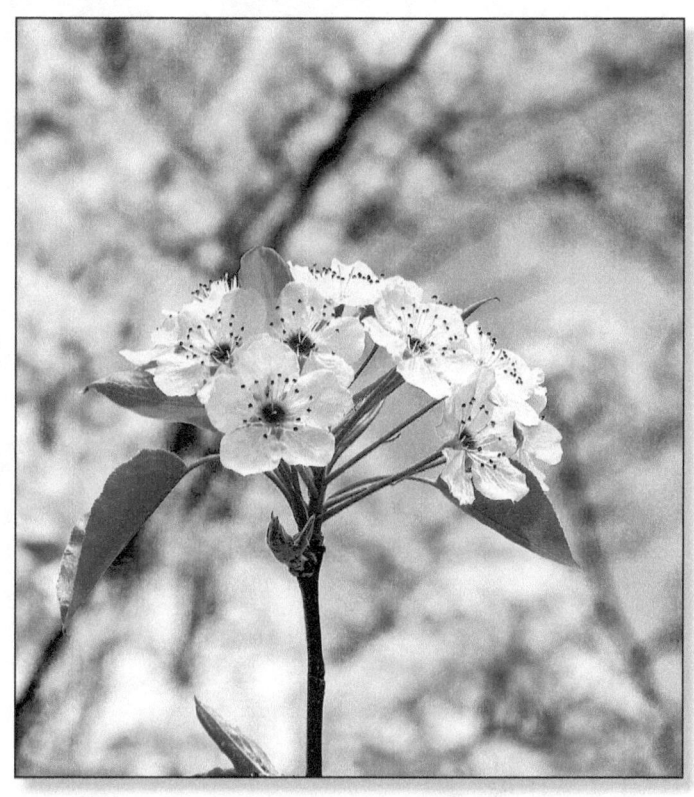

Saratoga Springs, N.Y., May 10, 2014.
Canon EOS 20D, 80 mm (128 mm), 1/320, f/10, ISO 200, P, pattern.
© 2015 by Shawn M. Tomlinson

be a little peeved about my recommendation of a camera it no longer makes or makes money from.

Oh well.

Certainly there are better cameras in existence than the 20D, but that does not decrease the usefulness of it. Personally, I'd rather have an older, well-built camera than a flashy new one made of plastic or sporting the "Rebel" logo. I know I can rely upon the 20D to produce fantastic images in a variety of circumstances, and, really, that's what a photographer needs.

All of the images in this book — except those of me — were shot with

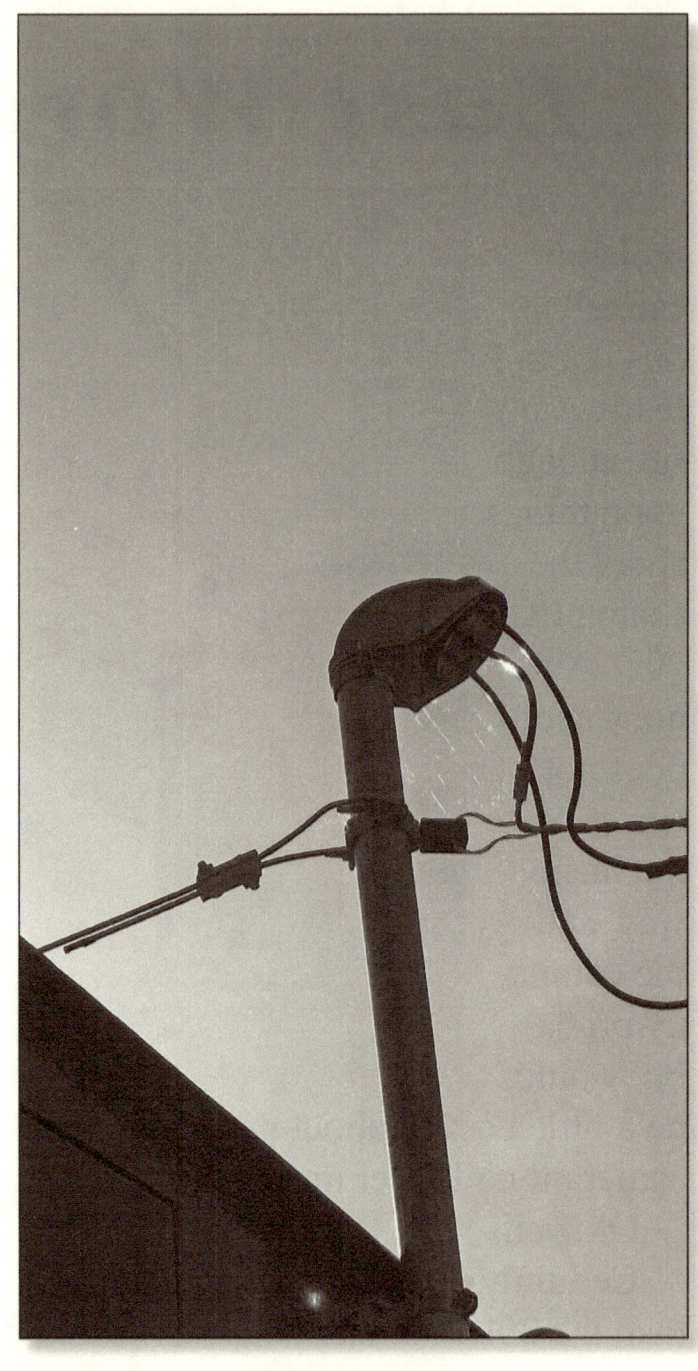

Freeman's Bridge, Schenectady, N.Y., May 12, 2014.
Canon EOS 20D, 97 mm (155.2 mm), 1/500, f/13, ISO 200, P, average.
© 2015 by Shawn M. Tomlinson

the Canon EOS 20D. Take a look at them and consider what the camera could do in your capable hands. (You can see the color images in the eBook version of this book.)

I've used the word perhaps too much, but you will be astounded.

—SMT, July 4, 2015

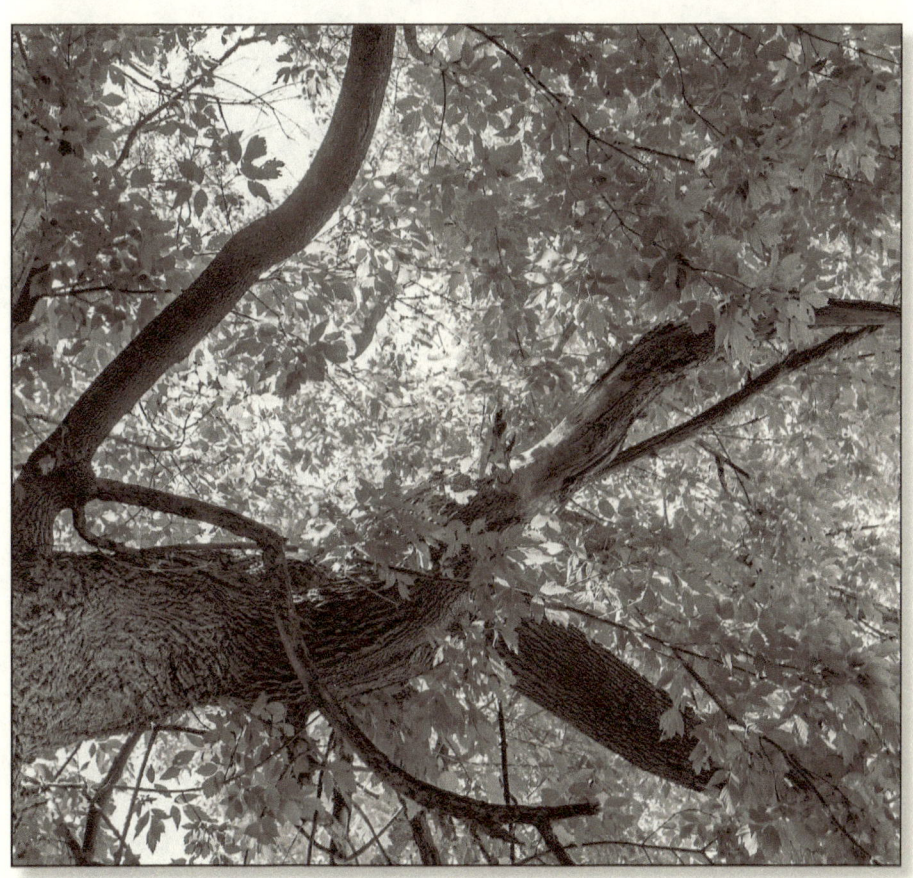

Clarksville, NY, June 8, 2014
Canon EOS 20D, 28mm, 1/80, f/5, ISO 200, P, pattern metering
© 2014, 2015 by Shawn M. Tomlinson

Shawn M. Tomlinson's Guide to Photography Series

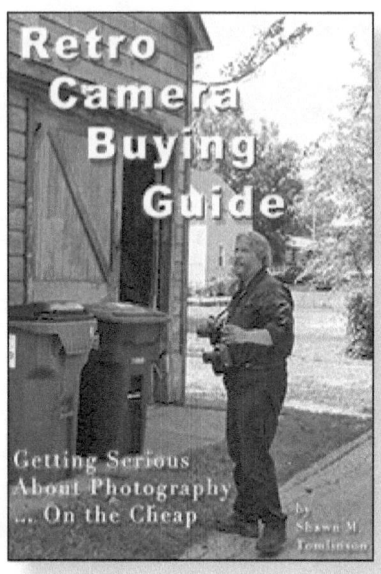

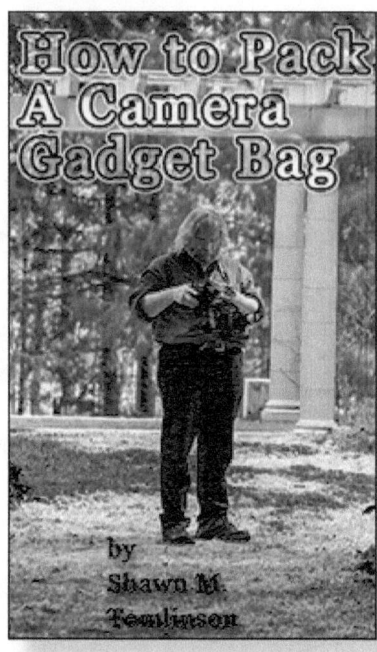

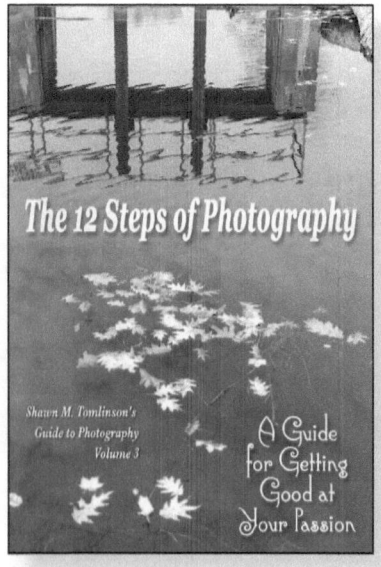

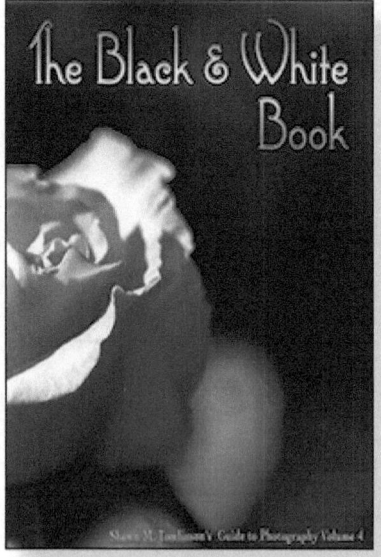

Shawn M. Tomlinson's Guide to Photography Series

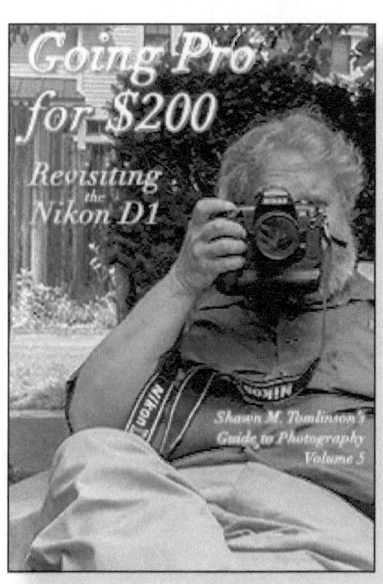

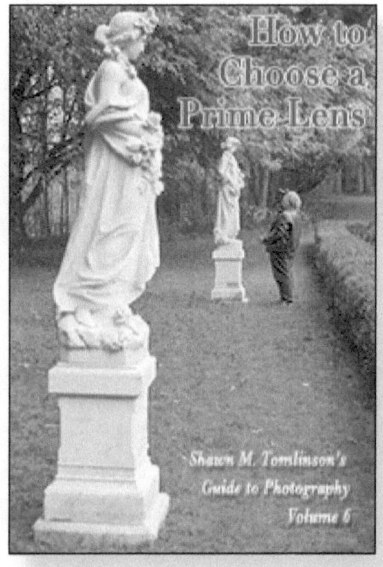

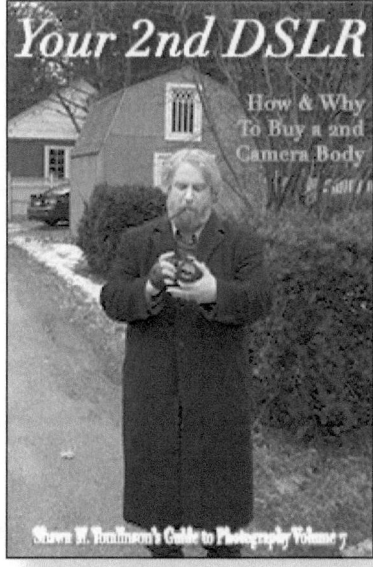

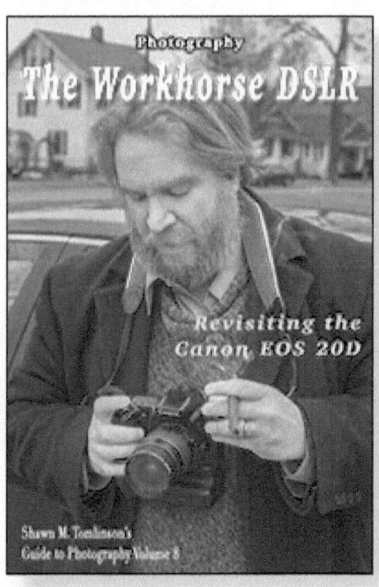

Shawn M. Tomlinson's Guide to Photography Series

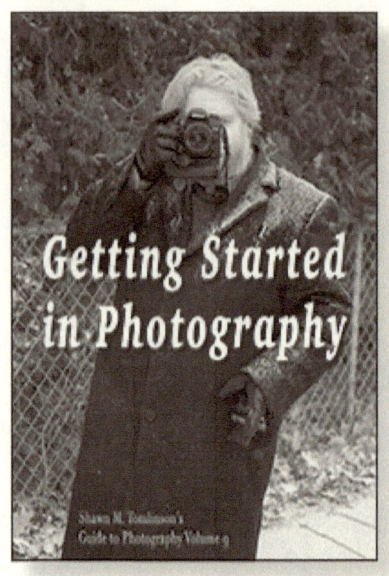

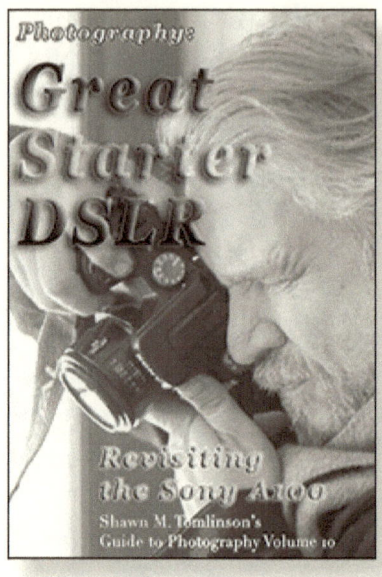

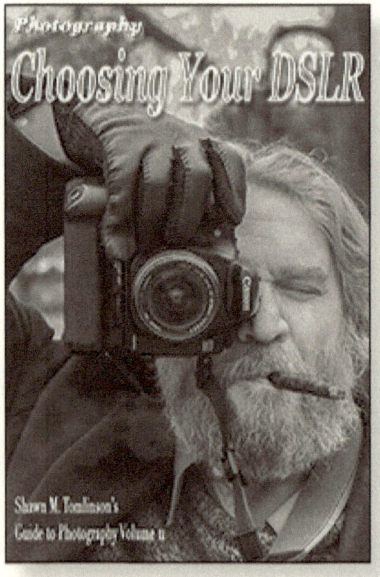

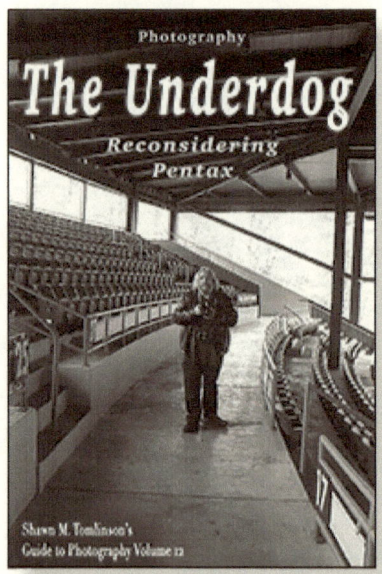

The Photo Curmudgeon

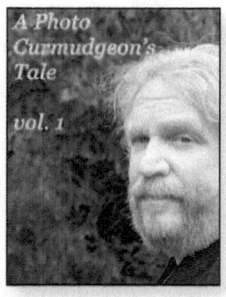

A Photo Curmudgeon's Tale
Volume 1 (eBook)

The first 25 Photo Curmudgeon columns collection covering everything photographic also includes several columns that preceded the Curmudgeon. Includes many photographs to illustrate points in the columns.

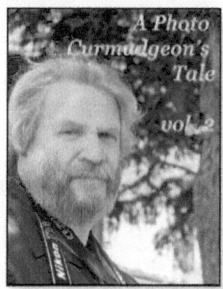

A Photo Curmudgeon's Tale
Volume 2 (eBook)

The second 25 Photo Curmudgeon columns collection covering everything photographic considers lenses, cameras, photo editing techniques, locations and more.

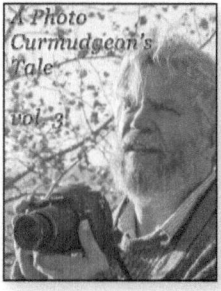

A Photo Curmudgeon's Tale
Volume 3 (eBook)

Photo Curmudgeon columns 051-075 are collected in this third volume covering everything photographic including lenses, cameras, photo editing techniques, locations and more.

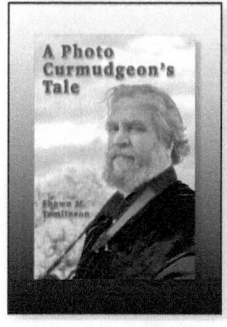

A Photo Curmudgeon's Tale
Omnibus (Hardcover & Trade Paperback)

A collection of the first 112 Photo Curmudgeon columns in hardcover and trade paperback formats. Available from Lulu.com, Amazon.com, Barnes & Noble and other outlets.

www.ingramcontent.com/pod-product-compliance
Lightning Source LLC
Chambersburg PA
CBHW022000170526
45157CB00003B/1073